12/25/03

To Our)
Dear Kristen
You are a wonder
teacher and we are so proud

Love,
Mom and Dad

Presented To:

_____

By:

_____

Date:

_____

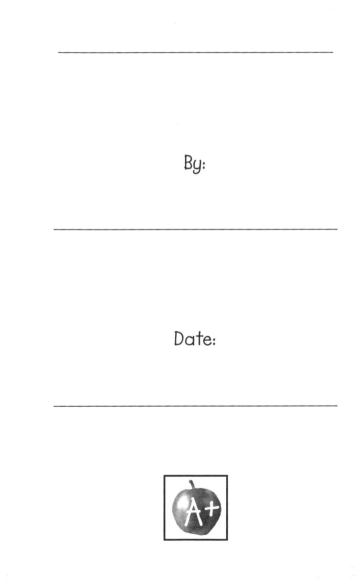

The Complete
apples &
chalkdust

Vicki Caruana

RIVER
OAK
PUBLISHING

The Complete apples & chalkust:
Inspirational Stories and Encouragement for Teachers
1-58919-013-0
Copyright © 2002 by Vicki Caruana

Published by RiverOak Publishing
P.O. Box 55388
Tulsa, Oklahoma 74155

Dedicated to Mrs. Robinson,
who inspired me in the first grade
to become a teacher myself.

Introduction

Once a teacher always a teacher—this adage is forever true. Most likely you were a teacher long before you ever set foot into a classroom. You were called. Then you heeded that call. Even those who came to teaching from an entirely different career were called. The talent to teach should never be taken lightly. We must nurture it, treasure it, and then shamelessly present it to the world with pride and commitment.

No one else understands what your days are really like except another teacher. That means we are each uniquely equipped to encourage one another. I realize that there is much to discourage us. I also know we've spent too much time waiting for society to wake up and appreciate us. I challenge you to step out of your classroom and reach out to another teacher in friendship, appreciation, and encouragement. The chains of isolation must be broken and the walls of territorialism must come down if we are to regain a sense of pride and joy in our calling.

This complete volume of *Apples & Chalkdust* stories provides you with at least one story to read each day of your school year. Take a moment before your students arrive in the morning and focus on this calling you've answered. Remember why you became a teacher in the first place and rediscover the joy that is still yours to be had.

And remember always, that you are where you belong.

Enjoy!

Vicki Caruana

"A teacher affects eternity; he can never tell where his influence stops."
—Henry Adams

Jay

Maggie pulled her four-year-old son's hand a little harder as she hurried him up the sidewalk. A black pickup truck had slowed alongside them.

"Who's that, Mommy?"

"Let's keep walking," Maggie said. Not recognizing the truck, she picked up the pace.

Just then her son tripped on a stray branch and pulled on Maggie to wait. As she stopped, the dark glass of the passenger window rolled down and a young man with sunglasses leaned over to get a better look at the sidewalk couple.

"Mrs. Jensen, is that you?" Maggie looked up, responding with caution to the distantly familiar voice. She scooped up her son and took a cautious step back from the street.

The driver stopped the truck, put it in park, and excitedly ran around to meet her. Taking off his sunglasses so Maggie could see him better, he said with a touch of disappointment, "You don't remember me, do you?"

Apprehension turned to delight as Maggie finally recognized her former student. "Of course I do, Jay. You're a hard one to forget."

"I never forgot you, Mrs. Jensen. You're the only one who gave me a chance."

Looking at him she could still see the twelve year old who fought the system. As the big, black truck rolled away, Maggie smiled as she read his business card, "Jay Getz, Architect."

Even if the results of your labor aren't immediately apparent, take joy in the fact that your influence reaches further than you know.

Your successes may not show up in the classroom. Sometimes they show up when you expect them the least and need them the most.

"Experience is not what happens
to a man. It is what a man does
with what happens to him."
—Aldous Huxley

Space Shuttle

Hundreds of squinting eyes focused upward on a cloudless Florida morning. Teachers gathered and waited along with their students for the show to begin. It's always great to bring the classroom outdoors. It adds a real-life quality to the lesson.

Finally, waving hands began to point toward the eastern sky. Applause and cheers built to a roaring crescendo. It was a proud day for teachers and students alike.

"Go, Christa, go!" they cheered.

The space shuttle, disappearing into the

atmosphere, suddenly exploded, and its expanding cloud of debris streamed to the waiting ground below. The applause turned to questioning gasps and disbelieving screams. Teachers hurried their students back into their classrooms like a mother hen gathering her chicks. The questions were many. The answers were nowhere to be found. Although crisis teams descended on every school, children continued to look to their trusted teachers for stability and comfort. Teachers became mothers, sisters, friends, and counselors.

Doing what they do best—they taught.

They reestablished routine, and they prayed.

Whether it's war, scandal, or tragedy, you cannot shut the world out of your classroom. Every once in a while, the world's classroom crashes into your own. Handled well, even tragedy can teach the most valuable lessons.

Teaching to the situation allows the situation to teach to you.

> "Change your thoughts and
> you change your world."
> —Norman Vincent Peale

First Class

Sandra had spent all weekend arranging and rearranging her classroom.

She decorated it with posters professing profound sayings. She set the desks in such a way that her students would receive the greatest impact from her teaching.

Finally, she sat on her stool at the front of the room and surveyed the setting.

It was perfect.

It had to be.

It was her first classroom.

Captivated by her own thoughts, she imagined

the events of the day to come. The student roster printed into her lesson plan book would come to life as the twenty-five sixth graders entered the room. The students, her students, would eye her warily as she moved to the front. She knew her carefully written name on the board would stump them. That was all right. She hoped its perplexing spelling would break the ice.

This was a moment she would remember all her life—a moment she had waited for and dreamed of since she was a little girl.

Sandra refocused on the still empty desks. With a heart full of hope, she prayed that this year would be filled with many significant and memorable moments for both her and her students.

What are your hopes and prayers?

On days when you wonder why you ever became a teacher, close your eyes and recapture the moment that inspired you long ago.

"The ultimate measure of a man is not where he stands in moments of comfort and convenience, but where he stands at times of challenge and controversy."
—Martin Luther King Jr.

Picket Line

Vicki was well prepared for her new teaching assignment. However, it's never easy to start midyear. Squeezing through the adolescent crowd, Vicki approached her room. She was abruptly stopped by a picket line!

"No new teacher!" the signs glared.

Twenty-five sixth grade gifted students paced in front of her classroom, unhappy that they had been assigned to a new teacher. Without hesitation, Vicki slipped between the protesters, pushed the call button to the office, and reported the disturbance. Gathering her materials from the desk, she began to write assignments on the board.

Just then her principal stepped in to let Vicki know that her students were on their way.

A deep breath accompanied by a quick prayer was all she had time for.

As the now subdued crowd reluctantly entered the room, Vicki welcomed them with a spirited "Good morning!"

Their defiant gazes only barely met hers.

"We've got a lot of work to do, so let's get started."

Passing out some neon colored paper she said, "I'd like to work with you on creative problem solving. First we need a problem. Any ideas?"

Reluctant hands went up, and so began the process of building a new class.

Sometimes the only defense for skepticism and doubt you will have is your own self-assurance and poise. But there's no better way to restore trust.

Try to turn every situation, positive or negative, into a learning experience.

"Our task . . . is not to fix the blame for the past, but to fix the course for the future."
—John F. Kennedy

Seize the Day

Teachers know that the influence of a negative home environment can sometimes overwhelm their own ability to influence students in the classroom.

You can spend endless hours and days devising just the right incentive program or learning strategy. You can look for every opportunity to offer praise. Still, you can do just so much good during the few hours you have with your students.

Then they go home and spend fifteen to eighteen hours out of each day there—some without nourishing meals, love, attention, or encouragement.

These are the children we teach.

Sound defeatist? Not necessarily.

Consider the influence a child's friends can have on him. Parents continually worry that their children will follow the wrong crowd. While they may spend a great deal of time with their friends, it is still less than they spend with you.

Your efforts have more impact than you could ever realize. So much of what people are, can be attributed to environment.

Teachers are a part of each student's environment.

Become the most positive, encouraging part of your students' surroundings. When you do, school can become a life-changing experience. Show students the higher ground—they might just decide to aspire to it.

Don't let your concern for tomorrow keep you from making an impact today.

"Do what you can, with what you have,
where you are."

—Theodore "Teddy" Roosevelt

Little Budgets

Jan sat on the floor of her make-and-take workshop trying to decide on the most crucial thing to complete. The calendar math chart was done. She had already started the flannel board. She had six more projects and only an hour left in the session.

"I'll just have to wait until next month," she commented to a fellow teacher upon leaving the workshop.

Jan knew that money was tight in her district. Her first year of teaching was full of the unexpected. Her $100 budget was a meager offering. She still didn't have enough textbooks. Students brought in their own supplies. Paper was a treasured commodity. Jan didn't know any different; this was her first year. All she knew was if she wanted something, she had to make it herself.

She learned how to shop smart when ordering from supply catalogs.

She learned to glean from the wisdom of more experienced teachers to implement ideas.

She learned to be resourceful with what she had.

Jan's students didn't give a second thought to all the handmade accompaniments in their classroom. They *did* notice a creative and innovative teacher who touched their lives.

Model for your students how to make the best of any given situation.

It doesn't really matter how big your budget is; what matters is if you are a good steward of what you've been given.

"Failure is only the opportunity to begin
again more intelligently."
—Henry Ford

Failed Lesson

John planned his study on multicultural
appreciation down to the letter. He gave his
students free reign when it came to presenting
their projects and envisioned all kinds of creative
multimedia presentations. With so many
interesting projects to choose from—he couldn't
wait to see what they would come up with.

Finally the day arrived and John began to call
the students up to make their presentations. After
five less-than-earth-shattering presentations, he
discovered that less than half of the class had
completed the assignment. It was obvious that this
was not just a typical situation.

Notes from frustrated parents were thrust in
his face.

What had gone wrong?

John decided to stop everything and find out why this lesson had become such an obstacle for his students.

He read the notes from the parents again and began to realize that he had overwhelmed his class with abstract guidelines and expectations. The idea was great. But John had to humble himself and admit to both the students and parents that he should have been more definitive in his expectations.

His humble attitude eventually earned him the loyalty of his students.

Allow creativity to define your projects, but be sure to clarify the guidelines for completing them. As a result, your students can exceed your expectations by courageously and creatively stepping out in their assignments.

If a great many of your students fail at some task, leave your pride at the door and look to yourself for solutions.

"Never, never, never, never, give up."
—Winston Churchill

Out of Time

At 6:00 p.m., Sally finally looked up from her computer screen. School was dismissed more than three hours ago, and Sally was beginning to feel the effects of skipping lunch. As the department head, it was up to her to complete an exhaustive report that had been sprung upon her at the last minute.

At 9:30 p.m., she called home to touch base and see if her husband had any trouble putting their two children to bed.

At 10:30 p.m., Sally was satisfied that the report was finally complete. She tried to print. She waited. Nothing happened. There was no ink in the cartridge.

Now what? she wondered. The office supply stores were closed. "Think Sally, think," she muttered to herself. Removing the computer disk, she hurried home. All the way she prayed that she would find an answer.

The next day Sally just couldn't focus on the morning routine. As she rushed to grab the car keys, her husband stopped her at the door. "Don't forget to drop this off," he said handing her the disk.

At that moment she realized the simplicity of the answer to her dilemma.

As Sally entered the school office, she approached her supervisor. "Here is the report you needed," she said as she handed him the disk.

As you work diligently, the most simple solutions usually reveal themselves.

You may not always be given adequate time to meet the expectations required of you. Work heartily. Stay focused on the task instead of the inconvenience it presents.

"The quality of a person's life is
in direct proportion to their
commitment to excellence."
—Vince Lombardi

Coaches

Ever wonder why coaches are so effective and
so loved by their players? *Coach* means *tutor* or
trainer. A good coach has high expectations,
encourages, and does more to "show" than "tell."

As teachers, we should take the opportunity to
learn from the efforts and focus of our school's
coaches. Coaches instill a sense of pride, a
cooperative spirit, and the competitive edge
necessary to win. Good coaches gain respect from
players and parents alike.

Good teachers run their game the same way. If

you want to lead a winning team, it's time you too became a coach. Yes, coaches sometimes have the advantage of choosing their teams, while teachers don't. But teachers, by inspiring students to achieve their personal best, have already won the game. Come alongside your students. Expect the best from them. Teach them never to settle for less. Spend more time showing and not just telling.

Your classroom is like the playing field. There are rules of play, scores to keep; there are victories, and yes, sometimes losses.

It's your job to train your students to perfect their game.

Take time to look at the winning team and find out what they do to win.

"One mother teaches more
than a hundred teachers."
—Jewish proverb

Frank Lloyd Wright

Frank Lloyd Wright's success as an architect
was a direct result of the influence from his first
teacher—his mother.

Like many of his contemporaries in the 1870s,
Wright was schooled at home along with his
siblings. His mother was always searching for
opportunities to advance and improve the
education of her children.

In 1876, the Wrights, taking advantage of the
special railway excursion rates, traveled from Boston
to Philadelphia to attend the Centennial Exposition.

At the Exposition, Mrs. Wright came upon a

life-affirming discovery for her son, Frank. The new Froebelian "Kindergarten" idea was on display, and Mrs. Wright eagerly drank in the new concepts and applied them to her children's education.

Although Frank was past kindergarten age, the Froebel ideas were quite formative for him, and he attributed much of his architectural success to his mother's wisdom and vision for his life.

As a teacher, never discount the incredible influence a mother has on her child's education. Allow her vision to reinforce your efforts in the classroom.

Strong parental involvement is key to the success of a child's education!

> Be grateful for parents who involve themselves in their child's education. They can make your job so much easier.

"Do the thing you fear and
the death of fear is certain."
—Ralph Waldo Emerson

Take Charge

Jayne's internship assignment in a high school seemed at first to be more intimidating than exciting. As she entered the school and forced her way through the crowd of 2,500 teenagers roaming the main hallway like an ocean of piranha, she felt sure she'd be eaten alive by the end of the first week.

Entering the classroom, Mrs. Randall graciously welcomed her and led her to a small desk on the opposite side of the classroom. "The kids will be here in about ten minutes. I believe in jumping right in, so as soon as the bell rings, you're on!"

Jayne's stomach was gurgling in protest.

Quickly arranging her materials, she stood at the front of the room and scanned the board for a piece of chalk.

The bell rang. She heard the shuffling of feet.

Jayne had no clue how to break the ice.

As frantic thoughts of what she should do or say next spun through her head, Jayne turned around just in time to see a paper airplane soaring by. She deftly caught the airplane in flight and without even thinking said, "Incoming!"

The students' critical stares immediately turned to grins of acceptance. With one confident move, she had captured the attention of her students.

And at that, Jayne relaxed and began to teach.

Remember that when you are put in charge— you must take charge.

"Encouragement is oxygen to the soul."
—George M. Adams

Balance

"Never smile before Christmas!" Most teachers know that there are some things you just don't do! And boundaries are a must when it comes to maintaining respect and order.

Common sense told Susan that it was easier to ease up on her discipline than to make it more strict. Yet, try as she might, she was unable to stick to that unwritten rule.

She loved children and wanted her kindergartners to have a sense of security.

She wanted her students to feel safe and to know that they could make mistakes without fear of humiliation.

She remembered well the embarrassment of having to stand with her nose to the chalkboard for an hour because she didn't know the answer to a math problem in junior high.

She did not want to produce that feeling in her students.

Susan believed, as so many teachers do, that part of teaching is to nurture. Students need to be encouraged to take risks and to grow in a learning environment where they feel safe. Susan understood that the love of learning is cultivated through encouragement, not fear.

As the year went on, Susan successfully ran a structured but creative classroom.

Keeping a good balance in your classroom can be a challenge. Let your students get to know you as fun and fair—but never as someone to fear.

Rule with mercy and grace, and your reward will be great.

"Creative minds always have been known to
survive any kind of bad training."
—Anna Freud

Einstein

Young Einstein was never considered a brilliant
child. Intellectually, he even seemed backward. He
learned to talk late. Little or none of his future
ability was detected in early childhood.

By age ten, he was considered precocious, but
in attitude only.

Even in high school, he was only considered
average at physics and mathematics. It wasn't until
Hermann Minkowski mentored him that his genius
was recognized.

After that, things began to change for Einstein.
His independence and self-confidence grew, so

much so that it was difficult for any university in the 1890s to satisfy him.

His spark of genius became fully ignited when he got a job in the patent office. Suddenly he saw the physical insights interwoven with the heavy machinery in the patent shop. It was there that Einstein's mathematical genius took flight. And history took one of its biggest leaps.

How often does genius fall through the cracks of the school system? Our challenge as teachers is to find creative ways to nurture independent thinkers and creative souls, encouraging them to reach beyond their imaginations.

Is there someone in your class today that could be, like Einstein, a diamond in the rough?

Provide for the gift of understanding and encouragement. You never know what gifts you'll allow to emerge!

"Be sure you put your feet in the right place, then stand firm."
—Abraham Lincoln

Pass or Fail?

Stan taught social studies at Melham Middle School for fifteen years and had the reputation of bringing history alive for his students. His students always seemed to thrive and do very well.

But each year he discovered more and more students lacking in basic reading skills, hindering essential comprehension.

"How did they get this far?" he questioned.

Two days before final grades were due, Stan had a conference with the principal. It seemed that two boys were failing not only his class, but every other class they were taking. The principal asked if

Stan could see his way clear to pass them.

This seemed stronger than a request, it seemed an expectation.

"I can't do that," Stan said. "They didn't pass. They didn't come to class. In fact, they did nothing!"

His principal still pressed. "They are too old. We need to pass them."

"Then someone else will have to pass them," rebutted Stan. "It's not fair to them or to the other students who worked so hard."

Although another teacher decided to give the boys a passing grade, Stan knew that he had done the right thing.

You may someday have to be the teacher who cares enough about the future of your students to keep them at the same level until they really learn.

There will be times when you must stand on principle, even when it is unpopular.

"If you judge people, you have
no time to love them."
—Mother Teresa

Soggy Leaves

by Tony Horning

Jamie came to school one morning with a rolled-up towel that secured his priceless treasure. Waiting to share was frustrating for both Jamie and Mr. Taylor. This little boy, eager to share his discovery, interrupted lesson after lesson.

When Jamie's time finally came, the students formed a circle on the floor. Jamie lowered his towel to the floor with such care and slowly unrolled it to reveal a handful of old, soggy, brown leaves from his yard—not the beautiful and colorful leaves of autumn with their vibrant reds and yellows; just plain, old, brown leaves.

As Mr. Taylor looked around that circle, he was surprised to see on the children's faces amazement, wonder, and joy!

Listening to the class you would have thought they were staring into the Grand Canyon. Captivated, these children held those soggy leaves as if they were newborn kittens.

There in that circle, the teacher became the student. For a brief moment, Mr. Taylor could remember a time when the simplest things in life brought wonder and joy to him as well.

Take time in your classroom to enjoy the simple pleasures.

If you miss the little things, you miss the vast majority of life.

"If a child lives with praise,
he learns to appreciate."
—Dorothy Nolte

Listen and Learn

Mary eagerly looked into the faces of her first class, fully expecting they'd look at her just as eagerly in return. However, eye contact wasn't easy to come by, and the only eagerness she saw was when they looked at the clock.

How do you compete with a clock? she thought.

Coming in behind another teacher in the middle of the year was hard enough. But coming behind a teacher who had been overly harsh made the situation even more complex.

Mary wondered if she would ever get past the wall that seemed so great between them. Their level of frustration, though unspoken, was immense. Her search for wisdom had only taken her to textbooks and research studies, but she did not find answers there.

One night, as she was unable to silence her thoughts in order to sleep—she made a decision that she needed to stop trying to fix her students and, instead, start trying to understand them.

She began to encourage her students in what seemed at times the smallest achievements, and invested much more time listening. By building up her students in their gifts and hearing them out on things, she created an amazing bond with them.

Even in her inexperience, she was able to find a connection with her students by simply showing how much she really cared.

What extra step can you take to connect with your students?

Take the extra time to get to know your students and show you care.

"Leave as little to chance as possible.
Preparation is the key to success."
—Paul Brown

The Best Laid Plans

Miss Sanders had worked all summer devising a myriad of plans she hoped would capture and delight her very first kindergarten class.

With wide eyes, her first students anxiously surveyed the classroom. They saw storytelling murals, expressive mobiles, and activity centers peeking out of every corner!

Miss Sanders told the children they could investigate any part of the room they wanted.

Billy couldn't even find a place to begin. He began to wander from station to station becoming more confounded by the minute. Miss Sanders didn't notice the lone explorer whose frustration was building. Finally, in desperation, Billy stood mid-room and bellowed in protest.

Miss Sanders rushed to calm Billy but was suddenly surprised by another tearful voice from the opposite side of the room. There began a growing whir of little people overwhelmed by their new surroundings—missing their mothers. Within seconds, the class exploded into a chorus of crying.

Neighboring teachers rushed into the chaos and calmly helped Miss Sanders round up and comfort the overwhelmed kindergartners. In moments, all was well again.

Miss Sanders was grateful for the others with more experience who came to her rescue that day.

If you are a new teacher, don't be afraid to ask questions or glean from the wisdom of seasoned teachers.

Look to the experience of others who have gone before you. They are there to offer comfort as well as guidance.

"Little by little does the trick."
—Abraham Lincoln

Give It Time

by Ailene Doherty

Amy was an enthusiastic and optimistic first grade teacher. By Thanksgiving her students were progressing even faster than she had hoped—all except for Jonathan.

Jonathan seemed so withdrawn. Amy wondered what she could do to make the classroom a happier experience for him. Maybe she could move his seat near children who would encourage him. Maybe she could offer him some sort of reward or assign him a mentor.

Then she was hit by a thought. Maybe she was trying too hard to change Jonathan. Perhaps he just needed time and patience. Amy relaxed and decided to give him room to progress at his own pace.

Only a few weeks later, Jonathan came during recess and handed her a book, "This is my favorite book. Would you like to read some of it to the class?"

An amazing improvement. His first step. Ever so slowly, the changes took place and by the end of the year, Jonathan was voted as the student who made the most progress!

There will always be students who take longer to adjust and fit in. Some times all they really need is time, patience, and to know you are available if needed.

It takes some children longer than others to rise to the occasion. Remember to give them time and not rush to fix a problem that may adjust itself.

All communities have a culture.
It is the climate of their civilization.
—Walter Lippmann

Environment

Laura is a teacher who is very self-confident and, to be honest, has a good right to be. She has a knack for accurately assessing situations. Unfortunately, her timing isn't always right, and she often runs into resistance.

This year when Laura started at a new school, she was excited and very much at ease even though it had been five years since she'd stepped foot into a classroom. Her enthusiasm and creativity spirited her to take on new activities and programs.

Laura was used to spearheading new ideas, but she wasn't used to a principal who was resistant to that kind of energy. She was stopped at every turn. Anything new was shot down. Her principal was comfortable with the status quo—no more and no less.

Laura's innovation had been squelched and her bitterness grew. Frustrated, she decided that this school was not where she belonged and impulsively put in for a transfer for the next year.

Even though it is a principal's job to get to know his teachers, it is just as crucial for a new teacher to take time to get to know the culture of his school. What is valued? What are the rules? Who has the power?

Being watchful, learning, and working within the parameters of your school's environment helps ensure your ability to make changes and adjustments later, when it really counts.

Learn your school's culture; adapt and become part of the mold before you try to break it.

"By learning you will teach;
by teaching you will learn."
—Latin proverb

Teachers are Students

As teachers, we are perpetual students. Yes, we may take another college course here or there to renew our certificates, but we also learn from our own teaching experiences.

Through the act of teaching, we learn how to resolve conflicts effectively. We discover how to talk so others will listen. We remember what it's like to be a student, so we tread with care.

Remember the first time you had to teach fractions and it wasn't until the end of the lesson that you finally grasped it yourself? That's not something to worry about; that's something to celebrate!

Experiencing the learning process along with your students provides you with wonderful insight.

Tell your students—they will know they've really learned something when they can teach it to someone else. Give them opportunities within the classroom to teach.

To educate is to be a part of a cycle of learning and teaching.

When you attend an eye-opening workshop, teach others what you have learned. When you make a mistake, encourage others not to do the same.

Have a humble heart when it comes to this business of teaching. You never know what you might learn or from whom you might learn it.

Don't be afraid to become a student of your students.

"Education is not the filling of a pail,
but the lighting of a fire."
—William Butler Yeats

Light a Fire

With the new standardized test of basic skills in place, teachers scrambled to stay on top of their curricula so their students would perform well on the test. The demands were great, and the time was quite limited. They found themselves teaching around the test—not the preferred way to teach, but it seemed to be a necessary evil.

Ken, a math teacher, was worried about a group of students who were falling behind. He had only six more weeks to complete multiplication, yet some students were still struggling with the beginning concepts. What could he do?

The time needed to go back and re-teach these

few just wasn't there. But Ken was not willing to accept the idea that some students must fall through the cracks, either.

He realized, just as King Solomon centuries ago, that knowledge for knowledge's sake is meaningless. He decided to focus his attention on inspiring his students with a passion for learning. This inspiration would reach far beyond any one test; it would prepare them for the test of life.

With this goal, he made the best use of the time he had. By adding enthusiasm, props, and visuals to his teaching during those last few weeks, he inspired a combustible hunger for knowledge within his students.

It's the fire you light under your students that matters. It filters through the cracks and reaches students at every level.

The fire you light in your students for learning will affect them for a lifetime.

49

"See everything; overlook a great deal;
correct a little."
—Pope John XXIII

Discipline

Discipline is probably the most talked about and most misunderstand aspect of education. Discipline comes from the Latin *disciplino*, which means *to instruct*. It's rooted in the idea of learning, not punishment.

Formulating a discipline plan is the first thing every teacher is expected to do, even before writing lesson plans. Each teacher has different discipline boundaries. And your discipline plan may be very original.

The process of adjusting to various discipline plans helps children learn how to adjust to the differing expectations of people.

Too much discipline can frustrate the learner. You are not called to frustrate or nit-pick. Devise rules that are simple, easy to observe, and fair.

The more rules you have, the more rules you must keep track of! And if you're not careful, you'll end up spending most of your time catching kids in their mistakes.

Choose instead definable boundaries, and become an overseer instead of a bounty hunter. Correct only when absolutely necessary, and make sure you follow through on every consequence.

Utilize natural consequences whenever possible. For example, if a child does not study for his test, he will fail. Natural consequences are easily understood and enforced. More importantly, they teach life-lessons which will be essential and valuable to students later on.

Good teachers pick their battles rather than picking on students.

"Don't limit a child to your own learning,
for he was born in another time."
—Rabbinical saying

Inclusion

Jan waited patiently as her department head worked his way through the team meeting agenda. It was the second time she had been scheduled to speak, but she had the sinking feeling they wouldn't get to her this time either.

Jan's learning-disabled students were struggling in the regular classroom environment—not because of their ability, but because there was a definite feeling of exclusion.

Jan needed to address this issue as an advocate for her students. After all, who else would speak up for them. Jan was willing to do whatever it took to change the way the needs of her students were perceived, but unless the team gave her a chance to talk, she wouldn't be able to make that needed difference.

Finally, it was her turn. Jan stuck to the facts, but not without emotion. Revealing her compassionate heart, Jan demonstrated to the other teachers what it was like to sit in a class where they were ignored, everything sounded garbled, and looked like nonsense.

As she made her final statement and returned to her seat, her team looked at her as if they had seen her for the first time. They were finally able to understand the helplessness her students felt.

Never allow an opportunity pass where you might be able to be an advocate for your students.

Remember that you speak for your students. Silence can be seen as agreement.

"They know enough
who know how to learn."
—Henry Adams

How to Learn

It wasn't until graduate school that Char learned how to learn. So much of her time in school had been spent memorizing meaningless facts. But in grad school Char learned how to think critically, synthesize information, and draw her own conclusions. She examined how she learned best and could identify different teaching styles easily. With this knowledge, all she had to do to succeed was to adjust her style when necessary.

Why does it take until graduate school before students learn how to learn, or better yet, how *they* learn?

Children have the capacity even as

kindergartners to recognize their own learning styles if they are shown how. Give your students the ability to discover their own learning styles, and their opportunities will be boundless. That awareness alone is power packed!

If you haven't taken a look at your own thinking and learning styles, you will not be able to help your students gain that same understanding. Take a chance and look inside yourself. You'll be pleasantly surprised at whom you meet.

Re-evaluate your *teaching style* by reflecting on your own *learning style.*

"In the arsenal of truth, there is
no greater weapon than fact."
—Lyndon B. Johnson

Revealing the Truth

"Honey, we need to stop at the office supply store. I need some things for my classroom," Sue said to her husband.

"What do you need this time?" he asked.

"The usual. Copy paper, black and red pens, legal pads, and some file folders."

"Can't you just get them from the supply closet?" he asked.

"What supply closet?" Sue laughed. "Once we run out, we're out. And it's too much trouble to get the bookkeeper to make out a purchase order just for some pencils. It's quicker to buy them myself."

When surveyed, teachers said they spend anywhere between $200 to $2,000 per year on supplies for their classroom. Teachers are accustomed to filling in the gaps. Sometimes teachers must even supply the basics.

Unfortunately, spending our own money can hinder the cause of teachers more than it helps. The budget crunch is not felt by key decision makers when teachers spend their own money trying to fix the problem themselves.

Try to remember, when tempted to supplement your classroom from your own funds, that your generosity may be masking budget insufficiencies that so desperately need to be revealed. Although it can be very inconvenient and frustrating, going through the wait or a little red tape reveals the need so things can be changed.

> Sometimes it's better to do without in order to highlight a problem to parents and administrators.

"I can live for two months
on a good compliment."
—Mark Twain

Compliment

by Ailene Doherty

Dr. McGuire was principal at Lackspoor High School. He was, undoubtedly, the most efficient person the teachers had ever worked with. He was, however, one of the most frustrating administrators on the staff. He never complimented them, neither did he criticize. He just issued bulletins stating what should happen and when.

After Alicia had been in the system for many years, she learned that Dr. McGuire's wife was very ill. She knew a sentimental card would not be appropriate to send to him. So she decided to bake her culinary specialty, an angel food cake, and give it to him. If he didn't approve of such a gesture, she couldn't be too severely punished, for she already had tenure!

Alicia's delight was unbounded the next day when Dr. McGuire handed her a ragged piece of a brown paper bag on which he had written a note that read, "You are not only a good cook, but a very good teacher."

Alicia went to her classroom, clutching her first compliment from her principal, marveling at the power of that small act of kindness.

The power of a genuine compliment is never wasted and is the best investment you can make in those around you.

Invest in your students, show your belief in them, compliment them, and acknowledge their gifts.

"Nothing in the world can
take the place of persistence."
—Calvin Coolidge

Perseverance

by Ailene Doherty

Jenny's tenth graders loved *Shane,* the little
novel by Jack Schaefer. And this novel became a
tradition she shared every year.

Two of the main characters are Joe and Marian
Starrett, homesteaders in Wyoming in the 1880s.
Joe labored diligently to clear their land. Day after
day he tried to uproot an old stump, wondering
whether he would ever conquer it. But one day his
perseverance paid off, and the stubborn old stump
rolled to his feet. Marian was just as determined as
her husband.

On one occasion, she forgot about an apple pie

she had put in the oven. That pie was ruined, but without hesitation she baked another one.

Jenny had learned many a lesson from Joe and Marian. Sometimes, when she had worked for hours on bulletin boards at school and still didn't feel satisfied, she would say to herself, "Keep at it; Marian did."

Many mornings, Jenny arrived at school early to help pupils with their essay writing. She became disheartened sometimes because a student who was an electronic whiz still found it difficult to express thoughts on paper.

But she kept trying and usually had the thrill of conquering her own kind of stubborn stump.

Stick it out with your students; there is no greater reward than to see a student finally break through and triumph!

If you give up, you give up on your students. They deserve your perseverance.

"If you want to be a leader with a large following, just obey the speed limit on a winding two-lane road."

—Charles Farr

Walk in Line

When Flora walked her class down the hallway toward the lunchroom each day, she was determined to teach them how to walk straight, tall, and with purpose in mind. She didn't want them wandering aimlessly down the corridor.

Flora expected her kindergartners to learn the right way to do things, and learning how to walk together in line was their first opportunity to do so.

When older classes would walk down the hall opposite her class and were rowdy and misdirected, she would point it out to her students. "See that class? Let's show them the right way to walk respectfully." Her students would proudly stand to attention, passing the older class with quiet sophistication.

New students to her class would be indoctrinated in line-walking their very first day. Flora would say, "Let me show you how it's done." And then she would walk forward leading her class like a mother duck leading her focused ducklings. Her students caught on quickly. It was truly a thing of grace and beauty.

Teachers are leaders. Lead your students on the right path by showing them what you want and how you want it done. Leading your students in the way that they should go begins with the simplest of tasks.

Let them see how *you* walk.

The way you travel through life is the most powerful legacy you can give your students.

"Motivation is when your dreams
put on work clothes."
—Parkes Robinson

Dreams

Lori could never understand the mentality
some of her contemporaries had when it came to
fulfilling their dreams. They believed that the
dream itself was enough. Lori was baffled at the
"someday I'll be discovered" attitude.

She had dreams, too. Lori dreamed that she
would become a teacher. So she put herself through
college. She dreamed that she would someday teach
teachers, so she got her Ph.D. She dreamed of
writing books, so she learned how, began speaking
at educational conferences, and was published!

Lori believed that dreams shouldn't just remain
dreams; they should become reality—knowing that

there may be those dreams that will always be dreams.

Lori also has a dream to travel abroad and be a missionary teacher, or to start her own school in the states. And as far-fetched and unreachable as that may seem to her now, it is attainable. It just means work and time.

What are your dreams?

If you think you've put aside your dreams, think again.

"I make progress by having people around
me who are smarter than I am—
and listening to them."
—Harry J. Kaiser

The Team

Upon becoming an administrator, Madelyn felt overwhelmed. Although she had trained for this position and had all the right degrees behind her, she knew there was more to it than that. She had to depend on the counsel of those already there.

The trick was figuring out on whom she could depend. After a few months of getting to know her staff, she knew it was not really "her" staff. They were still quite attached to her predecessor.

This arrangement could have hindered the overall progress of the department. Madelyn couldn't be the expert in everything. Curriculum was her strength, but scheduling was not. Parent interaction was something she reveled in, but a public image was not. She needed people who could fill in the gaps and make the team whole. Though at times uneasy, she had to depend on the strengths of her team.

As opportunities arose, either out of resignations or transfers, Madelyn's mission was to scout out experts.

By the end of the second year, she felt like she finally had a dynamic team of players in her department and found it easy to defer to their judgment. It became evident that leading where she was strong was expected and preferred by all those involved.

Even if you can't hand pick your staff, rely on the best of their abilities. When they shine, the team shines.

"You've got to continue to grow or
you're just like last night's cornbread—
stale and dry."
—Loretta Lynn

Spice It Up!

Are you in a teaching rut? How do you know?

Can you teach that algebra lesson in your
sleep? Be careful—you might be teaching while
your students sleep!

Strive to be a "seasoned" teacher—one who
doesn't lack vigor. A seasoned teacher is one who
brings variety, zip, and delight into the classroom.

Something that is seasoned wakes up the taste
buds and tempts the recipient to want more. Once
tasted, it is craved!

Do your students get excited by your teaching?

Do they want more?

How can you become seasoned instead of growing stale? What can you add to your repertoire that is unusual and interesting? How can you be surprising and tantalizing? You don't have to be a sideshow. You just need to bring your teaching back to life.

All around you are opportunities to do things differently. Send away for that catalog. Enroll in that class. Go listen to that speaker. Find your own personal zest!

Not only will your students be coming back for more, but you will enjoy your own teaching again.

> Spice up your
> teaching.
> Bring a new
> excitement
> into your
> classroom.

"When you make a mistake, admit it;
learn from it and don't repeat it."

—Bear Bryant

Learn from Mistakes

Natalie's previous principals had trained her to be a good teacher—one who accepted responsibility willingly and expertly.

Her move to the district office was one she welcomed and believed was the next step for her. Although she missed the classroom, she felt she'd be able to make a difference higher up.

Her first assignment as a resource teacher was to track down a missing camcorder reported stolen from a local high school. Natalie felt confident in her new position and, since the school's assistant principal was a former colleague, felt quite comfortable approaching him with this situation.

Unfortunately, as she began to question the assistant principal's handling of the robbery, her confidence was perceived as intimidation. She not only met resistance, but she also alienated the one person who could have given her answers.

Realizing her mistake she tried to apologize, but instead of seeming genuine, she came across as unprofessional. A complaint was filed, and Natalie was demoted to desk work the very next day.

Natalie jumped rashly into a role she thought had inherent power and respect. The truth is that power and respect are earned, not bestowed by virtue of the position.

When you are in a new situation, give yourself some time to learn the ropes and your decision making will be much more effective.

Take the time to learn the culture of your new environment before you act.

"It is sheer waste of time to imagine what I would do if things were different.
They are not different."
—Dr. Frank Crane

Reproof

Bob just couldn't get comfortable in his school environment. There were so many things he wished were different. To add to this he was the only male teacher on his team.

If there were more men here, he thought, *maybe I'd feel more a part of things.* He had been a math major in college and went into teaching as an afterthought. It was not his original intention, and he was uncertain in his teaching role.

Constantly he analyzed his situation for things that could have been done differently. And his colleagues tired of his constant deliberating on the matter.

Most of the time, the other teachers just quietly ate their lunch as Bob complained. One day Bob muttered, "If only things were different. . . ."

Finally, one of his friends spoke up and said, "But they aren't different. Get over it, and go on!"

Bob looked stunned, just as if he had been slapped across the face. After a moment, his face softened and he realized his friend was right. It was that very statement that enabled Bob to transform his perspective, move on, and enjoy his position as a teacher.

Hearing the truth can be painful, but try to remember a friend's reproof is rooted in love and can be an opportunity for change.

Things can be different only if you can make them different.

"If you don't like the road you're walking,
start paving another one."
—Dolly Parton

The Right Path

Patricia's mother was a teacher. Her grandmother was a teacher. Both of her sisters were teachers. Yet her mother encouraged her to do something else. She said, "You can do better."

To appease her mother, Patricia became a speech pathologist. She graduated with honors and went to work in a notable hospital for children.

After three years with different clients every hour and an environment she was uncomfortable in, she found herself dreading the start of each new day.

The symptoms of dissatisfaction surfaced. Patricia began to be chronically late. She withdrew socially at the hospital. She was tired all the time and began to hate the career path she had chosen.

One day, one of her young clients was about to be dismissed from her care. The parents asked Patricia if she would accompany them to a school meeting and explain their son's speech difficulties to the speech teacher there.

Patricia went willingly. She had always been curious about the school setting. After their meeting, she wandered the school soaking up its atmosphere thinking, *This is where I belong!*

The very next day, Patricia took immediate steps toward moving her career into the school system. For the first time in her life, she was content and fulfilled in her work. She had accomplished her own dream . . . she had followed her own heart.

Have you chosen your own path?

Have you followed your own heart's desires?

Make sure you choose your own path, and stick to it.

"A good deed is never lost;
he who sows courtesy reaps friendship,
and he who plants kindness gathers love."
—St. Basil

George Washington Carver

Whenever George Washington Carver tried to attend a school, he was quickly either turned away or ridiculed because he was black.

Following the Civil War, it wasn't easy for former slaves to carve out a life for themselves. Even so, George pressed on.

The Listons were a white couple whom George befriended while at Simpson College in Iowa. They owned a bookstore, and he spent most of his free time there. Later George chose to attend Iowa State, and once again he was the only black student. Immediately, he was the object of racial insults. In a letter to the Listons, Carver complained about the way he was being treated.

Mrs. Liston took the train to Iowa State and walked the entire campus on his arm. "The next day everything was different," Carver later explained. "The ice was broken, and from then on, things went very much easier."

Students who don't quite fit in for one reason or another sometimes just need a helping hand— not necessarily to help them reach but to help them connect.

Is there a student in your midst who could use your endorsement today?

Be an advocate for someone who really needs it.

"What is honored in a country
will be cultivated there."
—Plato

What Does Your Garden Grow?

Each school has its own unique culture.

A small school will look and function
differently from a large school. An inner city school
will look dramatically different from a rural or
suburban school. Elementary is different from
secondary; private is different from public.

Where the differences lie are not just in the
structures themselves, but in the values and beliefs
of the inhabitants.

Look deep into a school, and you can see what
is cherished. Walk the halls, and you will see what

they value.

Walk into a school that looks sterile with white blank walls, no signage, and complete silence, and you will feel like you have walked into a hospital. This school's leaders believe that students are there to be cured by their teaching.

Walk into another school with colorful walls, covered with students' artwork—where teachers' doors are adorned with their personal style, and you will see a school that values students' creations and teachers' personalities. It is a welcoming atmosphere, one that fosters growth.

Where do creative minds prefer to flower? They prefer a place where there is light, warmth, and plenty of food.

Is your school a place for growth? It could be! Begin with your classroom.

Decide today to be a tiller of the soil in your school.

"The secret of success is
constancy to purpose."
—Benjamin Disraeli

The Main Thing

by Tony Horning

As a student teacher, Carl was thrilled with all
of the fun and innovative things he had the
opportunity to introduce to his students.
Unbeknownst to him, his supervising teachers
were taking care of the plethora of other duties,
leaving him with a false perception of freedom as a
teacher. Before he realized it, he had given in to the
routine and lost touch of his sense of purpose.

As a new teacher, it isn't long before innovation
is traded for familiarity. Many a college graduate
enters their first classroom, finding there is far more
awaiting them than they could have ever imagined.

They discover themselves under an avalanche of paperwork from students, the principal, and the district. Creativity and enthusiasm can easily be squelched by the overwhelming and unseen demands of the classroom.

Eventually Carl realized his dissipation. He knew assigning and grading work wasn't teaching. He refocused his attention and developed healthy boundaries for himself, his students, and the daily pressing requirements. As a result, the flashes of brilliance and creativity once again entered his classroom. His students flourished and teaching again became his rediscovered passion.

More than anything else, students need you to be a leader who is able to reinforce the fact that they are worth more than all the homework you could ever assign.

Remember, the main thing is to keep the main thing the main thing.

"A true leader always keeps an element
of surprise up his sleeve, which others
cannot grasp but which keeps his
public excited and breathless."
—Charles de Gaulle

Open House

Tess inspected her room one final time before the parents arrived.

Students' work assignments were prominently displayed, and volunteer sign-up sheets were in plain view. The room looked both organized and creative. This was Tess's tenth open house night, but she still got butterflies as parents took their seats at the children's desks. She felt more on display than her students' creations.

This was her chance to make a good first

impression. It might be one of the only times she would see these parents face-to-face. She wanted it to be a positive experience—one that instilled trust and confidence in her ability to teach their children.

The room was packed—standing room only. Tess circulated the crowd, handing out a scavenger hunt she thought might break the ice. Within minutes children and parents were navigating the room looking for the places and things on her list. When at last everyone returned to their seats, Tess relaxed as she saw the smiling, excited faces.

It was a good start to a great year.

Putting forth the extra effort necessary to make parents feel confident about your teaching will produce enduring rewards.

Each year, show yourself to the parents as capable. Parents like to know that you are in charge!

"No act of kindness, no matter
how small, is ever wasted."
—Aesop

Conferences

Conducting a parent-teacher conference wasn't
covered in Sarah's education courses. Once a
teacher, she found that she was expected to meet
with each parent at least once a year.

Most of her students were doing exceptionally
well, with good grades and good behavior. But there
were a few who were frustrating. She was dreading
their conferences.

She started with easier conferences first,
secretly hoping that the parents of the more
difficult students wouldn't even show up.

After two or three conferences, Sarah noticed
that once she conveyed the positive things about

her students, parents responded with, "Please don't hesitate to let us know if Johnny ever strays." And Sarah wondered if the same might happen with the parents she was avoiding.

She called each of the parents of her most challenging students and told them at least one positive thing about their child. It wasn't easy, but it did force her to concentrate on the strengths of these students.

A few weeks later she scheduled their conferences. She repeated the positives and then enlisted help with the negative. She was encouraged to discover that these parents were just as willing to help and assured her that they would be supportive.

Not all of your challenges will be as easily solved. But remaining positive opens the door for parents to work with you toward solutions.

Tell parents the positive first. It makes the negative more palatable later.

"It takes seventy-two muscles to frown,
but only thirteen to smile."
—Anonymous

WYSIWYG

Sometimes the demands on teachers can be quite stressful.

In one day, you might be expected to fill out a mountain of paperwork, calm a tense parent, meet with your team about next year's budget, and . . . oh yes . . . teach!

The pressure of these demands can make it difficult to face the wide-eyed wonder in your students with enthusiasm day after day.

Your countenance speaks volumes. If your eyes are downcast or you stare with indifference when you teach, you cannot convey a love for learning to your students. But what if you just don't feel especially excited about vocabulary that day?

Scientists have found that even forced laughter has a beneficial effect, both mentally and physically. You may think that "faking it" is hypocritical, but sometimes in the midst of that forced smile, you actually do smile. A simple smile can change your attitude and recharge your teaching.

Don't forget "WYSIWYG": What You See Is What You Get. What are your students "getting" from you today?

Next time you feel nervous, tired, or stressed, indulge in a good laugh.

"If there be any truer measure of
a man than by what he does,
it must be by what he gives."
—Robert South

New Teacher

Jami was the newest teacher at Jackson Elementary.

Walking into the teachers' lounge her first day, she felt very much like an outsider. She sat at a table alone and unpacked her lunch. Within a few minutes the tables filled, and the room buzzed with discussions of kids, plans, and happenings of the day.

No one seemed to notice Jami.

Halfway through lunch, the principal walked in to notify another teacher of a phone call. She called to Jami before she breezed out the door, "Glad to have you with us, Miss Smith." Jami immediately felt more welcome and finally visible.

"Who are you substituting for today, dear?" a seasoned teacher asked.

"Oh, no. I'm a teacher here. I'm the new reading specialist," Jami said.

Suddenly, she was not only visible but on display. Those at her table seemed genuinely interested in her, asking her questions about her background and her thoughts on teaching.

How do you welcome a new teacher? When a new teacher arrives, assert yourself to do those things for others which would have made you feel more comfortable.

Try to remember how it felt when you were the new teacher.

If you're a seasoned teacher, take steps to make new teachers feel welcome.

"Don't find fault. Find a remedy."
—Henry Ford

Protective Parents

On first impression, Mrs. Gladstone was the parent most teachers dream of. She volunteered in the classroom two mornings a week. She was a partner in her daughter's learning.

However, as the year progressed, Mrs. Gladstone's involvement became overwhelming.

She started calling the teacher at home on the weekends. She was at her daughter's side for every field trip, whether she was needed or not. She began showing up for lunch every day.

While the teacher appreciated Mrs. Gladstone's intentions, she could tell Natalie was uncomfortable with her mother's constant presence.

The teacher tried to dissuade Mrs. Gladstone from coming on field trips and encouraged her to cut lunch dates down a bit. Mrs. Gladstone nervously refused the advice. She wasn't ready to let go.

Rather than causing unnecessary tension which could potentially damage the teacher-parent relationship, this teacher decided to change her strategy, including Natalie in group activities when her mother wasn't there. It took extra effort but in the end it was a win/win situation benefiting everyone.

In dealing with potential parental conflict, remember some of the best results can be derived from compromise.

Be gracious and understanding in dealing with parents, keeping in mind that they are entrusting you with their most treasured gifts.

"It takes time to save time."
—Joe Taylor

Be Prepared

Lesson plans are just that—plans. They don't just appear! Yet there are times when all teachers feel they don't have time to write down strategic plans.

Do you know teachers who "fly by the seat of their pants"—who always seem to be rushing around to gather materials at the last minute and aren't quite sure what page they are on until the kids tell them?

Granted there are too many things teachers have to do that have nothing to do with teaching. No one likes to bring work home. And a teacher's time is a precious commodity.

But the time spent trying to decide, *What are we going to do today?* is not yours. It's your students'.

Modeling time management and efficiency is an important part of the teaching process.

Your principal, fellow teachers, students, and your students' parents all watch how you manage your time. Your time management showcases your values and speaks your priorities.

What are you spending your time on today? How much time are you investing into those things or people that matter to you most?

Show your students that they matter to you. Come to class prepared!

"Blessed are they who heal us of
self-despisings. Of all services
which can be done to man,
I know of none more precious."
—William Hale White

Vocalist

Beth was considered the top vocalist in the choir.

The year had been hectic, and she didn't put her normal preparation into a difficult piece she was to perform for a major competition. Her life as a senior was incredibly busy, and she just didn't devote the time she needed in practice.

When her time came to perform, she forgot some of the words and didn't receive her usual high rating.

Beth felt awful.

Beth's choir director offered words of consolation on the bus on their way home. Those words only seemed to intensify the guilt she felt. She not only let herself down, but felt she had let her school down.

After the others got off the bus, Beth burst into tears. She sobbed with her head down, knowing she had not done her best. She felt a hand on her back and looked up to see her director with big tears in his eyes, too.

His tears brought healing to Beth's heart.

She knew by his words that he believed she could do better next time, but she knew by his heartfelt concern that he would be there to help her.

More than any other thing, your heartfelt and compassionate acts toward your students will lift defeated hearts.

Reveal your heart, and heal a soul.

"The heart benevolent and kind . . .
most resembles God."
—Robert Burns

Leo Buscaglia

Best-selling author Leo Buscaglia grew up in an Italian home. He actually learned English as a second language. Upon entering school, Leo was branded as mentally deficient, and recommended to be placed in a special class. He was "written off" by those who believed to know better.

Miss Hunt taught this special class. She was caring, warm, and paid little attention to the labels placed on her students. Miss Hunt modeled a love of learning to all in her class and saw Leo as rich in potential.

In Miss Hunt's class, Buscaglia blossomed, and after several months, Miss Hunt insisted he be re-tested. The results placed him into the regular classroom system.

Miss Hunt's door was always open to Buscaglia. She encouraged him and convinced him that wonderful things were in store.

Do you know a child who has been "written off" or "lost in the shuffle," by parents, teachers, or other students?

Perhaps you are the teacher, like Miss Hunt, who will give him or her the benefit of doubt.

A heart of compassion and belief can be the very thing that causes a student to "make it."

"An idea is salvation by imagination."
—Frank Lloyd Wright

Yelling

Susan's high expectations for her students sometimes led to some frustrating moments. She taught seventh grade, and found she was raising her voice frequently just to get their attention. Susan hated to yell. It wasn't in her nature, and it was extremely frustrating. Although it had some shock value, mostly it just gave her a sore throat.

Susan needed a better way to get her students' attention—something that would do the job without the stress. She always thought she had good control of her class. Now she wasn't quite sure. There had to be a better way.

Later that week she attended a workshop with

200 hundred other teachers. Many of the teachers hadn't seen each other in quite some time, and the initial visiting created quite a commotion.

The leader, impervious to the noise, announced in a normal voice, "If you can hear my voice, clap twice."

Then as the clamor decreased, "If you can hear my voice, clap three times." Suddenly the room was quiet.

That simple demonstration of control was exactly what Susan was looking for. She couldn't wait to begin applying it to her own classes that very next week.

Open your imagination to new and creative measures to capture the attention of your class.

Learn to diffuse frustrations by placing your energies into seeking positive, active solutions.

"Silence is not always tact . . .
it is tact that is golden, not silence."
—Samuel Butler

Gossip

Gossip can abound in a teachers' lounge.

If not careful, teachers can get caught up in scrutinizing each other's style, demeanor, or appearance.

Chad decided a long time ago that he would not engage in any deliberate attempt to slander a fellow teacher. Even so, he became an unwilling participant in some very destructive gossip. To the other teachers, his silence meant agreement.

He found out later that he had been maligned as well.

Chad was hurt and disappointed. He painfully

realized how loud his silence was heard and how misunderstood its meaning was. Plans for damage control raced through his mind as he chased vindication. What could he say? What could he do?

He needed words—but not words that declared his innocence—words of peace. Chad determined that day to use only words that would uplift and edify his colleagues. He decided to defuse them with kindness.

By resolving to disengage from the circles of gossip and speak kind words instead, you will win the respect of your colleagues. More importantly you could ultimately change the environment and team spirit of your school leadership.

Others will find little to gossip about if you stay busy spreading cheer, showing empathy, and teaching well.

"Between whom there is hearty truth,
there is love."
—Henry David Thoreau

Unprofessional Behavior

Jessica was a new, young teacher whose enthusiasm sometimes was in need of a bridle.

Giving compliments came naturally to her and she showered them on her colleagues whenever the spirit moved her. Jessica was also a very physical person who many times hugged teachers she especially appreciated.

She was particularly appreciative of the way Mr. Blue, the gym teacher, treated her kindergartners. He was loved by the students, respected by the parents, and had a winsome personality. Mr. Blue was also a handsome, married man.

Jessica's endless hugs and enthusiasm, albeit

well-intended, lacked professional boundaries. And talk of Jessica's behavior gave rise to many assaults on her character. It also caused wondering whispers about Mr. Blue.

Concerned, a close colleague sat down with Jessica and gently addressed the situation before it injured her career. Not only did Jessica accept the advice from her colleague, she was most appreciative.

Should you find yourself in a similar situation, check your own motives. Ask yourself, *Do I really want to help this person?* and if so, try to:

1. do no harm.

2. be sensitive, not superior.

3. keep your emotions in check.

4. depersonalize the issue.

5. be brief.

Sometimes the best way to show a person you value them is to lovingly speak the truth.

If your motive is really to help, you'll find a way to speak the truth in love.

"Education is helping the child
realize his potentialities."
—Erich Fromm

Jimmy

Jimmy challenged his teacher day after day.

The lesson was always interrupted to deal with some outburst or rule infraction. Mrs. Jenkins tried strict adherence to her discipline plan. She tried ignoring his behavior. She even tried bribing Jimmy. All these solutions were short-lived. They were Band-Aids when only holistic care would do.

As all teachers do, Mrs. Jenkins knew her students quite well. She knew Jimmy's likes and dislikes, strengths and weaknesses, gifts and talents. And she decided to try a combination approach that would address the whole child and not just his behavior.

Since Jimmy was artistic, Mrs. Jenkins gave him the responsibility of making posters. Since he worked better alone than in a group, she assigned him specific tasks at group times. And since he liked attention, she called on him for answers even before he could raise his hand.

In time, Jimmy's outbursts decreased. His productivity increased. Mrs. Jenkins had found a better way for Jimmy and for herself.

Try to always remember, your students are more than a set of behaviors. They are people who have needs, desires, and preferences. When problems arise, look past the situation and into the child.

Know your students well enough to identify what they need. Then give it to them.

> Choose not to label your students by their behaviors. Help them evolve into something better than they thought they could be.

"Though we travel the world over to find the beautiful, we must carry it with us or we find it not."

—Ralph Waldo Emerson

Dolphin Watch

Eileen's commute to school each day exhausted her. It took her over two bridges and through horrendous morning traffic. By the time she finally reached her classroom, she was usually frazzled.

She tried leaving home earlier, but because of where she lived, that didn't make any difference. She still found herself sitting on these bridges for an inordinate amount of time.

One Monday morning there was an accident on the bridge. Eileen actually took the car out of gear this time to sit and wait. It was a breezy Florida morning and the stretch of beach along the approach to the bridge attracted morning walkers. *I wish I could leave my car behind and walk along the beach myself,* Eileen thought.

Suddenly people were getting out of their cars and pointing to the warm Florida waters. Eileen slid out the passenger's door to see what the commotion was. A pod of dolphins were slicing through the waters just offshore.

Eileen was flooded with a sense of wonder and peace.

From that day forward, she saw the slow traffic as a chance to dolphin watch! And that simple observation changed her life.

In the fast pace of life, take time to smell the roses.

Remember not to get so wrapped up in life that you miss the beauty that is around you.

"The highest reward for a man's
toil is not what he gets for it,
but what he becomes by it."
—Ruskin

Meetings

There are times when it seems that schools
have become more like a place for teachers to have
meetings, rather than teach.

School improvement meetings, technology
meetings, parent-teacher meetings, and community
involvement meetings are carried on across the
country. It's easy to view these meetings and
committees as one more thing you, as a busy
teacher, don't really have time for. Then when the
meetings are conducted outside school hours and
infringe on personal time, you might even feel
confined and become frustrated or indignant.

Yet, what does an indignant attitude communicate to administrators, parents, and other teachers? Although tempted to think otherwise, these meetings go on to create a better atmosphere for our students in which to learn.

Perhaps you think your schools are fine just the way they are.

Perhaps you might take a closer look.

All organizations can stand improvement. Do you help the process?

You know the right thing to do.

The question is, "Do you love your students enough to do it?"

Quality schools are the result of quality teachers going above and beyond the call of duty.

"No one is useless in the world who
lightens the burden of it for anyone else."
—Charles Dickens

Encourage

Judith's decision to "job share" this year was
rooted in her desire to stay at home with her
newborn daughter, at least part of the time. This
choice wasn't working out as smoothly as she
had expected.

The baby seemed to be sick much of the time.
Judith never had enough planning time, and
teaming with her partner left much to be desired.
Most days she came to work exhausted and close
to tears.

It was a parent who finally noticed her anguish
and discouragement. This parent offered more than
just words of comfort; she offered friendship. You

see, she had walked in those shoes herself.

Judith got through that year, due in great part to the understanding and encouragement of a caring parent.

Teachers everywhere know the benefits of being an encourager to their students.

Everyone needs someone to cheer for them now and then. Don't let the extent of your encouragement end with your students. Fellow teachers need encouragement, too.

Is there a teacher on your staff who could benefit from your encouragement today?

"You cannot shake hands
with a clenched fist."
—Indira Ghandi

Turnover

Last year Joy found herself to be the only first grade teacher left on her team after an unprecedented number of other teachers transferred. These empty first grade slots were filled by teachers from four different schools, each with a different background and agenda.

Their first team meeting was the first time they had been introduced to each other. Joy wondered if she should have transferred, too. Joy's apprehension was mirrored in the faces of all four of the other teachers. There was an uncomfortable silence as they sat across from each other at the child sized activity table.

After a few minutes of polite introductions, Joy decided to jump in with both feet. "This can be either a miserable experience, or it can be the best year any of us have ever had." The teachers began to open up and share, each committing to making it work together.

That year became the best they had ever experienced. It was the first year of four dynamic years together.

The diversity of the group actually became its strength. For example: One teacher's experiences were from an inner city school. She knew a lot about high risk kids. So when any of them came across that kind of child, she became the "expert" and helped them handle the situation.

When conflict came, they worked through it and became a stronger team together.

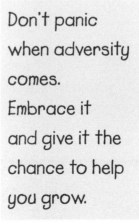

Don't panic when adversity comes. Embrace it and give it the chance to help you grow.

"Tact is the art of making a point
without making an enemy."
—Howard W. Newton

Accentuate the Positive

Carolyn wasn't quite sure when it all began. All she knew was that her tolerance for incompetence had diminished.

She was very concerned about one of her seventh grade science teachers. Mr. Roski's students were failing left and right. Students had reported that he typically sat at this desk reading the newspaper and looked up every so often to scowl at potential disrupters. He had become ineffective as a teacher and was so intense that even the parents were too intimidated to complain.

The bigger problem was that Mr. Roski had been at Jefferson Jr. High longer than anyone, including the administrators.

Carolyn knew that as principal, her actions, or lack thereof, would be testimony to her own effectiveness. She began to shine the light on those teachers who were doing exceptionally well. She even generated press releases to the local media about teachers and programs of which she was especially proud.

Parents began to request transfers into celebrated teachers' classes. This wave of positive energy didn't sweep Mr. Roski up—it swept him away. Actually, he jumped right off the boat and chose to retire early.

Many times it's more effective to accentuate the positives than it is to eliminate the negatives!

"Catch 'em being good" applies to both students and teachers.

"He . . . got the better of himself, and that's the best kind of victory one can wish for."
—Miguel deCervantes

Sweet Spot

In baseball, players talk of the "sweet spot." They describe it as hitting the ball in such a way that you know instinctively it's going out of the park.

Many athletes can relate to the sweet spot. Runners know when they run in the kind of rhythm that will win the race. Swimmers feel themselves slicing through the water toward victory. Olympic Gold Medalists will tell you the moment they knew they had won—way before they crossed the finish line!

Likewise as a teacher, you know what it feels like when a concept clicks. You see the lights go on in students' eyes and the wheels begin to turn in their brains. These are the lessons you allow to run over. These are the ones that even your most challenging students latch on to. These are the ones that make a lasting impact that your students will remember, even into adulthood. It's a feeling you crave to define your teaching.

It's not realistic to expect to teach in the "sweet spot" every time. Everyone has off days. But those athletes who know what it feels like, chase the security it provides.

What does it take?

It takes practice, commitment, and the desire to perform only at your best.

Decide today to do your best.

"Be a friend to thyself, and
others will be so too."
—Thomas Fuller

Birds of a Feather

Rob was accustomed to being the only male teacher in his school and craved camaraderie with teachers who were like-minded.

Sometimes there seemed to be too much negativity in the teachers' lounge. He longed to talk to teachers who looked at kids the way he did, worked the way he did, and considered parents the way he did.

During the past ten years, Rob had changed schools four times in search of a faculty with his same mindset. He began to wonder if he even belonged in the teaching environment. He considered going into another line of work, but he knew he'd miss the kids too much.

Rob decided to stick it out and put all thoughts about transferring again out of his mind.

After three years he finally befriended a new teacher at this school. They thought and taught very much alike and their friendship was fun and invigorating. Over the next few years, Rob began to meet at least one teacher a year whom he could talk with and exchange new ideas.

These tiny morsels of collegiality were rewarding and expanded his vision for teaching.

Just as the rewards of teaching may be few and far between, so may be the teachers after your own heart. But they, like those rare rewards, will be a powerful influence in your life.

Reach out and get to know your colleagues. You may discover a kindred spirit.

"Give to every other human being
every right that you claim for yourself."
—Robert G. Ingersoll

Labels

Teachers know the damage that can be done when a child is labeled. That label can remain with the child for years to come.

Whether for failings and inadequacies or even talents and achievements, labels do harm. They hinder children from excelling and believing in themselves and can even place undo stress on a gifted child.

Educational labels aren't limited to students. We can also get caught up in labeling fellow teachers, parents, leadership, and administration.

It can be as subtle as "She's the beginning

teacher" or "That child has difficult parents."

Whether the labels are spoken or not, the damage is done. Reputations are challenged. Perceptions are defined.

Just as struggling students need to be seen as students first, teachers need to be seen as teachers first.

Perception is reality for each of us. If you view your fellow teacher as lazy, then that's the reality of the situation to you. If instead, you choose to view that person as a teacher who needs help staying motivated, you can now relate to him or her, and even help touch their life.

Decide today to challenge your own perceptions; you might really make a difference in another's life.

Labels belong on cans, not people. Can you find it within yourself to clarify your view of others?

"What comes from the heart,
goes to the heart."
—Samuel Taylor Coleridge

Support Staff

It takes a lot of people to make a school run. The staff includes teachers, administration, kitchen staff, custodians, building maintenance, and the list goes on.

If you are new to a school, introduce yourself first to these critical groups of workers.

This is not to say that there aren't kitchen workers who yell at the kids too much or head plant operators who disappear when there's work to be done. This is just to say that without them your job would be much more difficult.

The growing sizes of our schools dictate that

we hire more support staff. Just as you can't keep your car running without a mechanic and fuel, you need support staff to help bring to life all you aspire for your students.

Go out of your way to get to know the support staff at your school. Offer tokens of appreciation periodically. Speak kindly to and about these people. Offer words of encouragement and compliment them in front of others.

Your boards will always be cleaned, you'll be served an extra helping of your favorite lunch, and you will also build up relationships within your school. Most importantly you will be teaching your most valuable lesson to your students—respect for others.

> Model for your students, respect for others and team spirit.

"No one can make you feel inferior
without your consent."
—Eleanor Roosevelt

Student or Teacher?

Sharon felt intimidated on her first day of internship.

At only twenty-one she was about to walk the halls of her rival high school from her own school days. Strangely enough, it felt all too familiar.

The huddled bodies outside the cafeteria. The frenzy of the first bell. The wooden desks all in a row in lecture style. She felt like a student standing there in the front office, her assignment in hand, waiting to see the principal.

After some quick introductions and a lackluster tour, Sharon hurried to her first class. Her pace quickened as she approached the main hallway.

Then, like a shot in the dark, she heard, "WALK!"

Sharon turned to apologize before entering the classroom. Then she thought to herself, *Hey, am I the teacher or the student?*

Later that day, she entered the teachers' lunchroom. As she navigated the ala carte line, she was abruptly stopped by a teacher whose voice she recognized from earlier that day.

"Young lady, what are you doing here? This is for teachers only."

"I'm not a student," Sharon replied, standing tall. "I'm an intern here."

"An intern! Well, I suggest you try harder to look like a teacher. I couldn't tell you apart from our students."

Sharon replied politely, "I'm sorry if I offended you. But the fact remains that I am an intern and I do belong here."

Deflated, the blunt teacher returned to her place in the line.

Overlook intimidation. Stand tall in the position which you have rightly earned.

"God gave man work, not to burden him,
but to bless him, and useful work, willingly,
cheerfully, effectively done, has always been
the finest expression of the human spirit."
—Walter R. Courtenay

Mirror, Mirror

Tim couldn't remember why he went into teaching thirty years ago. Whatever the reason, it was lost to him now.

He was looking forward to the next few years, only because they would lead out of education and hopefully into something more fulfilling. His apathy was visible—not just to his fellow teachers, but also to the students themselves.

To his colleagues Tim was distant and uninterested. He rarely interacted on any social level. Even cordial greetings were usually met with no more than a groan.

To his students, Tim barked out assignments with all the subtlety of a Marine drill sergeant.

His actions and attitude spoke volumes to his students. Tim communicated through his behavior that teaching was a lousy job and intimidation a powerful motivator. His students came to know classwork as punishment.

What a testimony!

What testimony do you give your students? What work ethic do they see you model in your teaching? What have they learned from watching you?

Self-reflection clarifies better than any mirror.

"One of the best ways to persuade
others is with your ears."
—Dean Rusk

Listening

Have you ever had a conversation with
someone whose responses weren't in response to
your thoughts, but to his own? You know the kind
of person who can't wait for the other person to
stop speaking so he can say what he wants to say?

Steve had the strongest personality on the
textbook selection committee. His opposing points,
which he made frequently, reminded his colleagues
of a lawyer's closing arguments. He was logical,
rational, and a problem solver. However, he
alienated everyone on the committee and usually
intimidated them into reluctant silence.

Steve, as a result, became frustrated with the

committee's lack of enthusiasm. He tried to rally them to a consensus on the issues, but all he perceived was ambivalence.

In actuality, Steve had talked himself right into isolation from the group.

With characteristic passion, he finally said, "We're getting nowhere. What do you want from me?"

Matter-of-factly, one member answered, "A chance to get a word in edgewise."

From this embarrassing experience, Steve learned an important life lesson.

When working on a team effort, think positive and seek resolve in solution oriented terms.

Be honest with yourself and evaluate. Are you being a team player?

"There's only one corner of the universe
you can be certain of improving and
that's your own self."
—Aldous Huxley

Show and Tell

Beth was known for her innovative teaching. She had been chosen "Teacher of the Year" just the year before.

She had become popular and was known for obtaining grants that secure monies to enrich and enhance the educational experience for her students. Sure that others would want to share in her luster, she suggested and offered a workshop for those teachers interested in doing things along a similar vein. She would teach them all she had learned.

Her principal approved, and Beth announced her workshop at the following faculty meeting.

One week later, she stood in her classroom

watching the clock, realizing that no one was coming to her meeting. Just before she packed up for the day, a friend came to see her.

"Are you here for the workshop?" she asked hopefully.

"No. I came to see how it went."

"Well, I guess everyone had other things to do, because no one showed up," Beth said matter-of-factly.

"I'm sorry. Maybe next time you could make it more like a social, and they'll come."

"I wasn't here to be sociable!"

Beth knew as soon as the words left her mouth that her attitude had been all wrong. No wonder no one had shown up for her meeting. She had isolated herself from her colleagues.

Determined to not let that same attitude of pride dictate her behavior again, she nurtured and shared her secrets with her fellow teachers on a personal level and regained their trust and mutual esteem.

If you find yourself frustrated with others because they are failing to meet your expectations, check your own standing first.

"Statistics are no substitute for judgment."
—Henry Clay

Number Crunching

Each year standardized test scores are used to determine whether or not students are succeeding. Districts publish reports ranking their schools according to test performance. Deciphering these statistical reports is difficult at best.

Tim and his family were moving to another city and their realtor had sent him the breakdown of scores on the surrounding area schools.

The reports were complex. He could tell which schools had the highest reading and math scores, but he couldn't tell which schools had the most innovative and caring teachers.

Tim wanted his children to attend a neighborhood school, without having to ride a bus. He wanted them to feel safe, yet part of a bigger community.

With his report in hand, he selected five specific schools and decided to take a trip to visit them. Tim made his final judgments based on the following criteria:

1. Which schools had friendly office staff?

2. Which schools allowed him to freely visit the classrooms?

3. Which schools had principals who were found more often in classrooms than in their offices?

Tim's final choice was a school that ranked good in test score standings but also high in the other things that mattered. Tim's children thrived there and were very happy with the choice their dad had made.

Remember that teaching is more than high test scores; it is also enriching lives.

"The best things and best people
rise out of their separateness;
I'm against a homogenized society
because I want the cream to rise."
—Robert Frost

Dare to Be Different

The quest for equity dilutes the power of diversity. You can see it all around you. Every child gets a trophy whether they win or not. Competitions are only disguised showcases of mediocre talent. Everything is designed to ensure the satisfaction of as many as possible.

Standing out for your accomplishments isn't "in." It might make someone else look bad. In some places, going above and beyond the call of duty is actually discouraged.

Are you creating a homogenous classroom? Does the high achiever feel he or she can shine, or is his or her talent shrouded amidst the average?

When we create the same boundaries for everyone, we are ignoring individuality and unique gifts.

Admittedly, in this world of quotas and demographics, it is hard to stand up for diversity.

But think about it. As a teacher, do you believe all teachers should be granted the same rewards? Are you intimidated by the idea of merit pay or teacher-of-the-year awards? Do you scowl at the new teacher with bright ideas? If so, ask yourself why.

Instead of letting your fears paralyze you, let them light a fire of inspiration under you.

Rise to the occasion and dare to be different! Allow some individuality in your students. Only then will you discover their true potential.

"The secret of success is
constancy to purpose."
—Benjamin Disraeli

Stick to Your Goals

It's easy to get distracted from your mission as
a teacher. Your time is limited and the demands
are great.

Good teachers are always on the hunt for new and
better ways to do things. You want to make the lesson
more exciting for your students and for yourself.

Sometimes a change of pace or style can have a
great impact.

Have you ever attended a conference or
workshop that was particularly innovative and
exciting? Did you learn strategies or a new
program that seemed to have S-U-C-C-E-S-S

written all over it?

We all know from experience that just because it's new doesn't mean it is better. And just because it is different doesn't mean it will work.

How can you judge whether or not this new idea is worth trying? Ask yourself these questions:

1. Does this idea inspire me?

2. Will this new technique blend cohesively with my teaching style?

3. Can I incorporate this idea into the classroom and still accomplish my goals with students, or will it become a distraction?

Change simply for the sake of change isn't enough. You need to clearly see a direct connection between the strategy or program and your aspirations for your students.

"Although the world is full of suffering,
it is full also of the overcoming of it."
—Helen Keller

Annie Sullivan

Helen Keller was considered a sort of wild child before Annie Sullivan came to teach and work with her. Her world now dark and silent, Helen thrashed around the house much to her parents' dismay.

After a slow and frustrating start, Helen recognized her first word in sign language—water. It was a triumphant day for both teacher and student.

Soon after, Helen was quick to learn other words. Annie was proud of her student. She could not believe how quickly Helen learned. She called her progress a miracle. Helen's accomplishments were amazing, achieving what seemed to be impossible.

Now that Helen could express her thoughts, the crying fits stopped. She was happy and contented.

Whenever Annie taught her a new word, Helen would throw her arms around her teacher and kiss her.

Teachers of delayed or disabled students can testify to similar miracles. Parents usually bestow undying gratitude to the teacher who unlocks their child's world and gives them hope.

Each child's potential can be unlocked. Each teacher has the key. Are you willing to take the time to find out which key fits?

Your undying commitment may well be met by undying gratitude.

"My business is not to remake myself, but make the absolute best of what God made."
—Robert Browning

Growing

If you've been teaching the same way, under the same conditions for a long time, then burnout could be a possible reality.

And just as you encourage your students to never stop learning, you too must continue to develop, grow, and enrich your life in ways you might have never considered.

If your attitude toward workshops is that they just take you away from your classroom and are not that valuable, then it is time for you to seek out other opportunities for growth.

Commit to attending at least one educational

conference a year, whether you get paid for it or not.

Join an area association and pour over the journals and materials that come with the membership.

If you don't have time to take a university course in current trends and issues, then at least go to the university bookstore and buy a title that looks interesting.

If you feel like you've just been treading water for a few years, decide now to take the plunge. Sometimes you have to immerse yourself into educational and community events in order to feel a part of things again.

A good start is to spend time with teachers who talk about education instead of the ones who complain. Before you know it, you'll remember why you went into teaching in the first place. The love affair can begin again.

Daily make an effort to grow and become your best.

"It is impossible for a man to be made happy by putting him in a happy place, unless he be first in a happy state."

—Benjamin Whichcote

Are You Happy?

Jan's previous school was new, full of the latest technology and innovative teachers. She longed to go back, but she didn't have enough seniority.

Jan was miserable at Jones Elementary. This school was old, small, and full of teachers who were from "the old school." Her frustration grew until finally she decided to leave.

Moving to a new district was full of promise. Since her new school was located in the state's capital, she thought the emphasis on quality would be evident.

But again, due to lack of seniority, she was placed in a school in a low socio-economic area that was old, rural, and full of teachers stuck in their old routines.

"I want to go back to my old district," she cried to her husband. "They were more professional there."

Jan continued to move from school to school, never satisfied. The fact was that even in her first school, she wasn't happy either.

The bottom line is that Jan just wasn't a happy person, and geographical relocations and new circumstances were never going to change that issue. Jan had never had the self-discovery that true personal happiness comes from within.

Take a look at your world. Are you content? If not, take a look inside. Are you happy with who you see?

Attitude is everything! If you are unhappy with where God has placed you, look inside your heart.

"If a friend is in trouble,
don't annoy him by asking him if
there's anything you can do. Think of
something appropriate, and do it."
—E.W. Howe

Friends

Cindy and Sharon were expecting a baby at the same time this school year. Because they were friends, it made it all the more special.

Then one day Sharon didn't come to work. She had miscarried over the weekend. Cindy's sadness for her friend turned into apprehension as she wondered what to say once she returned. She knew she'd be a constant reminder to Sharon of her loss.

When Sharon did return, she walked like a ghost through the school's hallways. No one spoke to her, let alone acknowledged her loss. They didn't know what to say, so they said nothing. Even Cindy found herself avoiding her friend. She knew Sharon was hurting; she just didn't know what to do about it.

Two weeks later, Cindy happened upon Sharon in the teacher's lounge during her free period. Sharon was supposed to be in class, yet she was here, crying. Cindy instinctively comforted her friend, but then realized Sharon's class was unsupervised.

Sharon was paralyzed with grief and couldn't function. Assuring Sharon that everything would be all right, Cindy ran to the classroom just after the late bell.

Cindy took care of Sharon's class that period. It was all she could think to do, yet it was just what Sharon needed from her.

Use compassion when dealing with fellow teachers, and act swiftly when duty calls.

Never use words when action is required.

"There are only two lasting bequests
we can hope to give our children.
One of these is roots; the other, wings."
—Hodding Carter

Louisa May Alcott

Louisa May Alcott was a teacher's kid.

Her lively temperament suited her father's unorthodox teaching methods during the 1830s.

Bronson Alcott had started several schools during Louisa's childhood. Louisa spent much time in her father's schools, even before she was of school age herself. Some of her fondest memories were of playing in her father's schools.

Bronson Alcott believed in making lessons as exciting and interesting as possible. Alcott's schools always started out quite promising, but because people did not understand his new methods of education, many grew uncomfortable and withdrew their children from the schools.

But for Louisa and the students who were allowed to remain, their futures were transformed. Bronson Alcott brought the elements of adventure, curiosity, persistence, and creativity to his students as part of the learning process.

Louisa learned how to give of herself before others as she watched her father sacrifice for teaching.

His love for teaching touched her deep inside. His support for her writing gave her fledgling career wings.

As teachers, never bridle your enthusiasm for teaching in front of your students. Let them see you boldly go forth to shape minds and mold futures.

Transform futures with adventure and creativity!

"Imagination is more important
than knowledge."
—Albert Einstein

The Right Answer

"What would it be like if . . ." Miss Chandler asked her wide-eyed sixth graders, ". . . if we suddenly had to live without electricity?"

Silence. No hands rising. Questioning looks.

"Come on," she coaxed. "Just yell out ideas." Again, silence.

"Okay, I'll start you off." Miss Chandler proceeded to list three things they would have to do if they didn't have electricity anymore. Slowly but surely, the students sat up a little taller, and the answers started coming.

Afraid that they didn't have the right answer,

her students were reluctant to participate in the creative process.

Schools have trained students that the right answer is the one that matters most. So what you see on students' faces when you ask thought-provoking questions is usually fear!

How can you make your classroom a safe place to dream?

It's more than creative bulletin boards and playing classical music in the background. It's your attitude.

If you believe that there is value in the process, then you must communicate that to your students. They have to know they can give a wrong answer in order to find the right one. And they need to know that sometimes there is more than one right answer.

Most importantly, they need to know that there will be times in life when no answers are available, but seeking for them is always okay.

Is your classroom a safe place to dream?

"A good laugh is sunshine in a house."
—Thackeray

Laugh

Justin was the class clown. There wasn't a day that went by that he didn't interrupt some lesson with his quick wit. He saw "funny" written all over everything.

You have to be careful with the class clown. He or she can easily take over your class and Mr. Watkins had decided early on that this would never happen in his class.

But it became a challenge to Justin to make Mr. Watkins laugh. Justin realized that it had to be carefully planned. He also realized that it could happen more easily if he completed all his work so Mr. Watkins wouldn't have anything to complain about.

What Justin didn't know is that Mr. Watkins was struggling every day not to laugh. He didn't want to give Justin the satisfaction.

But Justin was hillarious! The more Mr. Watkins avoided eye contact, the more Justin attracted attention to himself. It was becoming a stressful situation for Mr. Watkins. He began getting tension headaches and would end the day in a grumpy mood.

Then one day it happened. Mr. Watkins let go and laughed out loud!

The class was shocked; the clown was jubilant!

The teacher was relieved.

Headaches gone, Mr. Watkins realized that laughter really was the best medicine. He decided to take a dose each day.

If handled well, laughter can be used to your advantage.

Let them see you laugh, and you let them see your heart.

"Every child is an artist.
The problem is how to remain
an artist once he grows up."
—Pablo Picasso

Dr. Seuss

Ted Geisel's talent for writing and drawing didn't always impress his teachers. Once in art class, the future Dr. Seuss turned his painting upside down to look at it. He wasn't exactly sure why he did it, but he found out later this is how an artist can check a painting's balance. If the painting is balanced, it will look good upside down or right side up. His art teacher, however, thought Ted was fooling around and claimed that real artists never turned their paintings upside down.

"That teacher wanted me to draw the world as it is," Ted said, "and I wanted to draw things as I saw them."

Ted rejected his art teacher's advice not to pursue art as a career. He resolved right then and there to be an artist someday.

Even though he was shy, uncoordinated, and had a unique sense of humor, his stubbornness is what pushed him into the spotlight.

What does an artist look like? He may not be the pretty one, the graceful one, or the evident genius.

He may be the one you least expect to succeed because he follows the beat of a different drummer. Listen for that offbeat, and pay closer attention to the drummer.

Encourage the artistic soul discovered in your students.

"A place for everything, and
everything in its place."
—Samuel Smiles

Order! Order!

Teaching is one of the few professions that if
you're absent, an immediate replacement must be
found for you.

It takes more than written substitute plans for
a stranger to effectively teach your class in your
absence. It also takes organization.

Do you know a teacher whose room is one big
pile? Whose desk isn't evident to the human eye?
Whose supplies spill into crevices and corners and
whose files are in name only?

That teacher puts a substitute in peril when he
or she takes over a class.

How can a teacher help a substitute? Leave directions. Let the substitute know where the teacher's manuals are. Where the grade book is. Where the supplies lay hidden.

When substitutes have to rely on students in order to find things, then they appear helpless. They aren't able to adequately cover the material and take control of the classroom. They feel frustrated and may never come back.

Teachers complain that they are not considered professionals by the world.

How professional is your classroom by the world's standards? Your room is a direct reflection on you.

Need help getting organized? Find someone whose classroom you admire and ask for help.

"Treat people as if they were what
they ought to be and you help them to
become what they are capable of being."
—Johann Wolfgang von Goethe

Reach for the Stars

Barb was used to having children with special
needs in her fourth grade classroom. She knew how to
modify the curriculum to fit her students individually.

Parents were appreciative of her open-
mindedness, and their children succeeded in
her class.

One year, Barb was faced with a child whose
needs she had never encountered before.

Chris had one of the highest IQ's she had ever
seen. He scored four years above his grade level on
standardized tests. But Chris had become lazy, and

would only do the bare minimum. Even so, his bare minimum was still higher than the rest of his class. He got straight A's, but Barb knew he could do more.

Barb decided to raise the bar on Chris. She defined for him a separate list of expectations. At first Chris balked at the change. His comfort level was threatened. For the first time in his short academic career, Chris wasn't sure he'd get an A. He had to work for it.

After a few weeks of careful monitoring, Chris had regained his passion for learning. He began to crave challenge, and Barb gave it to him. She kept him on his toes, and he kept her on hers.

Never let your students accept the status quo. Push them; let them taste the satisfaction and exhilaration that come from a hunger for knowledge.

Teach your students to reach, and they'll never stay on the ground.

"The good life, as I conceive it,
is a happy life. I do not mean that if
you are good you will be happy—I mean
that if you are happy you will be good."
—Bertrand Russell

Babe Ruth

A few months after his seventh birthday, George (Babe) Ruth was labeled a juvenile delinquent and was sent to the St. Mary's Industrial School for Boys. The years he spent at St. Mary's turned his life around.

At St. Mary's, George had to follow a strict regimen of activities that included religious instruction, academic studies, industrial training, and athletics. George, of course, excelled on the athletic field.

But it was more than athletics that saved George Ruth.

Brother Matthias took the boy under his wing and encouraged him to take advantage of his talents. Matthias was a fair man. George, who was considered one of the school's biggest trouble-makers, respected him. Matthias, who was responsible for putting Ruth on the right track, gave George the love and attention he never got from his own father.

Ruth later said that Brother Matthias was "the greatest man I've ever known."

Is there a Babe Ruth in your classroom? A troublemaker whose talent has yet to be harnessed? You know who he is. He's the one you wish would be absent, but never is.

Maybe you will be the teacher to point him or her in the right direction.

Give your students a chance, and they might well make you proud.

"Nothing has a better effect
upon children than praise."
—Sir P. Sidney

Positive Reinforcement

George felt like he was in a no-win situation.
They cut his position, and the only way he could
stay at his school was to take a new position as a
dropout prevention teacher. He really didn't want
to, but he felt like he had no choice.

He was miserable, and it showed. Other
teachers commented that George's classroom was
like a morgue—cold, sterile, and much too quiet.
George got through the curriculum and kept order.
But the day could never end soon enough for him
or his students.

Then one day George received a letter from a
parent. He cringed upon opening it but found

instead a treasure. This parent was incredibly grateful that her son was finally learning and that there was a teacher her son could count on.

The letter completely changed George's outlook. He felt appreciated.

For the first time that year, he smiled upon entering his classroom. Not surprisingly, his students smiled back!

As a teacher, you appreciate affirmation from others, because it sends the message that you are reaching your students and doing your job well.

You know how well you do when you're complimented; don't forget to share the wealth with your students.

"The rain falls on all the fields,
but crops grow only in those
that have been tilled and sown."
—Chinese Proverb

Success

Teacher in-service is a necessary evil.

With so many changes being implemented, it's difficult to stay up on what is expected. Training is demanded and budgets are crunched in order to meet the needs.

Workshops take up almost every free moment. When you sit in an auditorium full of hundreds of teachers (who would rather be somewhere else) and learn about a promising new strategy, have you ever noticed that only a few actually carry out the recommendations?

It depends on whether or not a teacher is returning to a school that values innovation and embraces change. It depends on whether there is an administrator who frees up teacher time so they can employ new approaches. It depends on the needs of the teacher.

How similar is this phenomenon to what happens in your classroom every day? You teach a new concept and only a small percentage latch onto it right away.

The future success of your students will depend on whether or not you have created an environment that welcomes questions. It depends on whether you give them the time they need to master topics. It depends on whether you're meeting the needs of your students.

Set your students up for success, not failure.

"People should be free to find or make for themselves the kinds of educational experiences they want their children to have."
—John Holt

Teddy Roosevelt

None of the Roosevelt children went to public school. When they were little, their aunt taught them their lessons. As they got older, tutors were hired to educate the children.

Mittie Roosevelt was devoted to her children, and also instilled a strong spirit of adventure and daring in them—especially young Teddy.

This was particularly important since Teddy suffered from more than his share of illnesses.

His asthma made it impossible for him to take

part in the lively games the rest of the family enjoyed. He spent much of his time alone. But Teddy was bright and inquisitive, so his mother encouraged him to spend his time reading and writing. His mother's devotion as his teacher gave Teddy a well-rounded education.

His love for nature was fed by books and first-hand meetings of real-life explorers. His thirst for adventure was fueled by his mother's provision and made him the rough-riding president history recorded.

Do you know a child whose parents have decided to school him at home? Instead of being defensive about their choice, do what you can to make it the best choice possible. Offer your expertise and ideas. Be a help.

You know the commitment it takes to be a teacher. Respect the parents who make that commitment themselves.

"Until you try, you don't know
what you can't do."
—Henry James

In the Spotlight

Candice was a teacher who wanted to be an integral part of her new school. She had experience in yearbook, chorus, and writing. So working with these clubs would be natural for her.

Weeks after the school year began, a teacher left unexpectedly. Not only did she leave a hole in the language department, but now they needed a new drama club sponsor.

The principal approached Candice with the job, since she knew Candice was looking to get involved. But Candice had no experience with drama. She was reluctant to take on such a big job.

Her principal encouraged her to try. She could always quit if she wanted to, so Candice tried.

What she found out was that she loved drama! She was good at directing. Her organizational skills and attention to detail made that year's production one of the most professional the school had ever done.

When the students presented her with a dozen roses at the end of opening night, Candice couldn't believe she was standing on stage being applauded for efforts she never knew she could bring forth.

When you find yourself in the spotlight, even if you were pushed there, you may find you like it and actually deserve to be there.

Some of the best discoveries are made when we simply try.

"Try to say the very thing you really mean,
the whole of it, nothing more or less
or other than what you really mean.
That is the whole art and joy of words."
—C.S. Lewis

Words

Deborah was easily intimidated by parents, especially those who were the most vocal. Fearing the way a principal might view her, she avoided a documented parent complaint in her records at all costs. Deborah followed the path of least resistance and ignored minor student disturbances.

Her conferences were always a mere formality. If a problem was avoidable, she'd avoid it. A certain situation, however, changed her perspective.

A colleague's child was in Deborah's advanced

math class. Never expecting this to be a problem, Deborah was quite surprised that the student was not performing to the class standard. In fact, he was failing. Upon checking his records, she found that he actually belonged in another class.

She met with the mother and fellow teacher about the situation, only to discover that she had manipulated the situation and purposefully placed him in that class.

After going 'round and 'round for an hour about what help the student needed, Deborah decided to cut to the chase. "What I mean to say is that Steven really belongs in an average class."

As expected, her comment didn't go over well, but the information was received. They came to terms and moved him to the correct class, and as Deborah expected he excelled.

Following professional ethics sometimes takes courage. What's the alternative?

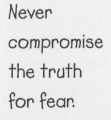

Never compromise the truth for fear.

"Work is love made visible."
—Kahlil Gibran

Love Your Job

Ellen knew she wanted to be a teacher since the first grade. She could remember setting her bedroom up like a classroom and making her four siblings be the students.

Her first grade teacher, Mrs. Robinson, loved her students. They in turn loved her and loved to learn. Ellen wanted to instill that same love in others, so she became a teacher.

All agree that teachers don't get paid enough. You have to be in it for more than money. You have to love to teach.

Ellen always felt on fire when she was teaching.

When a lesson clicked, it was an exhilarating feeling.

Once in a while she'd give students a chance to teach the class. They knew the material well enough to make a presentation. Those who volunteered did so out of desire, not out of outside pressure. She could see future teachers among her students. She could see their love for learning.

So when the union couldn't negotiate a higher raise or the budget was cut again and her materials were meager, she was still happy.

Ellen was doing what she loved, and she did it well.

Remember to teach from your heart, not from duty.

When you do what you love, you do it well, no matter the circumstances.

"There is no greater delight than to be conscious of sincerity on self-examination."
—Mencius

Support

Laura was new to teaching. Vicki was a veteran teacher and had been at Lake Elementary for many years.

Vicki took it upon herself to show Laura "the ropes" of their school. She pointed out its strengths as well as its weaknesses. She provided inside information on the school's culture, took Laura under her wing, and they quickly became good friends.

New ways of doing things defined Vicki's teaching style. She was a creative fund-raiser, a strong student advocate, and an excellent communicator with parents.

Laura was learning much from Vicki and was especially appreciative. But she was uncomfortable with Vicki's critical nature of others.

It quickly became evident to Laura that the other staff members were noticeably uneasy with Vicki's critical nature, as well. Laura knew she needed to talk to Vicki about her aggressive quest for excellence, yet felt awkward approaching the subject being the "new kid on the block."

Timidly and reluctantly, Laura spoke with Vicki.

Vicki's silence made it difficult to tell how she was handling the insight. But after a few days of soul-searching, Vicki returned to Laura and said, "Thank you for your honesty. I was looking at the other teachers as 'them' instead of 'us.'"

In teaching it is important to remember that your colleagues can be a great support system. Support them in all things.

Be a supporter of the team, not an opponent.

"People only see what they
are prepared to see."
—Ralph Waldo Emerson

Do It Your Way

Teaching eighth grade science was Susan's passion. She effectively covered the content and inspired her students to ask questions. Most days she could be found at the center of huddled eighth graders who were trying to catch a glimpse of some scientific phenomenon.

Her supervisor, Mr. Dawson, was from "the old school." He saw disorder when students crowded around her. He saw unprofessional conduct in her enthusiasm. He didn't see what he expected to see: students working quietly, and a teacher lecturing from the overhead projector.

During a conference, the assistant principal warned Susan of his forthcoming evaluation. She muzzled her disbelief as she strained to maintain the appearance of professionalism.

Realizing that it was his perception that her students weren't learning, she knew she had to prove otherwise. Calmly, she explained her philosophy and invited him to return the next day to her class.

That next day, she carefully orchestrated a lesson that showcased her students' grasp of a scientific method. They performed beautifully as if on cue. Once Mr. Dawson was satisfied, Susan was free to teach her own way.

Fair or not, there will be times in teaching that you too will have to satisfy the doubts of others and prove yourself.

Sometimes you need to give others what they want before you can do what you want.

175

"Take the attitude of a student. Never
be too big to ask questions. Never
know too much to learn something new."
—Og Mandino

Involuntary Transfer

Jan's involuntary transfer to an elementary
school was difficult. Not only did she prefer middle
school, but she felt inadequate to teach at that
level. Just because she was certified in elementary
didn't mean she wanted to teach it.

Teaching in a self-contained classroom all day
was quite an adjustment for Jan. Her first method
of coping was to keep to herself and observe.

After the first grading period, she realized there
was more to being an elementary teacher than
wearing theme jewelry and giving out stickers. Her

demands on her students were too high and she knew it. She could tell from their faces when she assigned research reports. She could tell from their parents as note after note came in with complaints. She just didn't know what to do about it all.

During her third grade team meeting, Jan sat and listened to Kathy, a first year teacher. Kathy's students loved her. Her room was bursting with energy and creativity. Even her discipline problems were minimal.

How does she do that? Jan wondered. Then in a moment of utter humility she said it aloud, "How do you do that?"

That was the beginning of a beautiful friendship and a successful school year!

Don't be afraid to ask questions of team members you admire or to share tips with someone new.

Find someone who is doing what you want to be doing well, and ask them how they do it.

"The important thing is
not to stop questioning."
—Albert Einstein

Why?

You encourage your students to ask questions. You tell them that the only stupid question is the one that's not asked. You try to create a non-threatening classroom environment in which students feel safe to ask questions.

There is a question, however, that you cringe at when you hear it: "Why?" A question that disputes the choices you've made about what to teach can put you on the defense.

Contrary to popular belief, questioning the status quo is not always disrespectful. There are times when it causes a teacher to stop and think—to question oneself.

How often do you evaluate how you're doing in the classroom?

Forget the annual evaluation your principal conducts. Ask yourself what you're doing and why you're doing it.

In turn, question the status quo at your school. Look for relevance in every decision. Look for pertinence in every choice. If you are on a committee, don't be afraid to ask, "Why this fund-raiser? Why this time? Why this way? Why this reward? Why this trip?"

Ask the questions everyone thinks about but never has the courage to speak. Ask the hard questions.

Ask, "Why?"

Define your goals; then every once in a while ask yourself, *Am I on track?*

"Act enthusiastic and you
become enthusiastic."
—Dale Carnegie

Power of Positive Thinking

Cecile made a deal with her seventh grade class on the first day of school. She said, "I'll warn you when I'm having a bad day, so you warn me when you're having a bad day. That way, we'll both give each other a little extra grace."

This system of mutual respect actually worked in the beginning. If Cecile had a particularly bad morning, she would announce, "I got very little sleep last night and I'm grouchy."

By the same token, a student would say, "I had a fight with my mom this morning; I'm not in a good mood." Each side would then give the other a wider berth.

Unfortunately, this plan began to backfire. She noticed that more and more kids were complaining. They were all concentrating on the negatives in their lives. Even students who were usually upbeat began to complain about their day. It had all gone too far.

Cecile decided a new approach was in order.

She pushed "smile and the world smiles with you" instead. It took a lot of patience, but slowly the class took on a more positive attitude and their performance improved.

What positive imprint can you leave on your class today?

Reinforce a positive attitude within your students.

"Shoot for the moon. Even if you miss it you will land among the stars."
—Les (Lester Louis) Brown

Expectations

The challenge of motivating students occupies much of a teacher's time and resources. Constant thoughts of, *If I could just get into their hearts, I know I could get through to them.*

You hope they care enough to try and excel. You certainly want them to excel!

It took until graduate school for Anna to realize the power of expectations.

Her professor told them that he expected to see only A's and B's out of his students. He spelled out what to do to get a *B* and what to do to get an *A*. Assuming they all wanted A's, he went into the greatest detail, outlining specifically how to get one.

Could this work in my classroom? Anna wondered.

To her amazement the first time she tried this, a quarter of her students expressed the desire to work toward an *A*. Three-quarters chose to work for a *B*.

By the end of the year, more than 80 percent of her students actually achieved higher grades than they did the period before!

This exercise in expectations was triumphant—for both the students and the teacher.

Keep your expectations for your students high. Mix those expectations with large doses of encouragement and you will discover a class full of achievers!

Never underestimate the power of expectation.

"There is a great man, who makes very many feel small. But the real great man is the man who makes every man feel great."
—G.K. Chesterton

The Note

Joyce could never do anything to please Mrs. Raymond. After three years at Charter Middle School, she walked the halls in timid avoidance of her principal. Three humiliating observations and conferences made Joyce feel insignificant and insecure.

The next year another principal was transferred to their school, and like before, Joyce avoided contact with her.

Then one morning, Mrs. Baker, the new principal, popped her head into Joyce's room. She took a seat at the back of the class unnoticed by the students, and stayed for the entire lesson!

Joyce worried. This observation was unannounced. She was sick at the thought of what was to come.

Later that day, Joyce found a note in her mailbox.

"Thanks for a delightful morning. It always encourages me to see a good teacher in action. Keep up the good work!"

This small act of kindness encouraged Joyce and several other teachers like her, to stay on at the school and continue to perform their best.

A change in principals almost always generates some staff turnover in a school. Those who fell in line with the previous administration are apprehensive about the changes that are sure to come. Yet most times, change is good.

Try to keep an open mind regarding change. Don't let your fears hinder bright possibilities.

Remember how you benefit from simple acts of kindness and bestow those same gifts on your students.

"Behind every able man there
are always other able men."
—Chinese Proverb

Alone

Susan sat alone in her classroom eating her
lunch as she did every day. The only sound was the
clicking of the ceiling fan which was the only
means of relief on this sticky May day.

Her students loved their innovative and creative
teacher. She could turn mundane facts into lessons
of real life intrigue. She could motivate unwilling
children in a single year. And when she was
nominated "teacher of the year," no one was
surprised. But just like Superman, this super teacher
felt very much alone amongst her colleagues.

Susan was not the only exceptional teacher at her
school. She was just the one who gained the most

attention. Attention from the local media. Attention from supervisors and from students' parents.

Then why does she dine alone each day? Peer jealousy. It infects even the best of schools. It can destroy healthy relationships and kill morale.

How do you reverse its effects? One way is by reaching outside of yourself to others. Another way is to esteem others above yourself.

You can't create a shared vision by being a lone ranger. Remember to include others in your plans, and they will remember to include you.

> If building yourself up is tearing others down, then it's time to rethink your priorities.

"If you don't say anything,
you won't be called upon to repeat it."
—Calvin Coolidge

The Tyrant

Judy had been looking forward to this school year with great anticipation. Prior to that first day, she tried to speak with her new principal. As school social worker, she needed to know what Mrs. Ricker expected from her.

After three unreturned phone calls and two unsuccessful visits, Judy decided she would wait until she saw Mrs. Ricker that first day.

Just before lunch Judy was called into the principal's office. "Miss Wilson, we have a problem."

Before Judy could even respond, Mrs. Ricker continued, "I expected you to contact me personally before ever setting foot on my campus!"

Judy sat there in confused silence. "How could the district send us such an inexperienced social worker?"

The only thing Judy could do now was to pray that her composure would remain intact. She turned to leave, but Mrs. Ricker's words pursued her. "And if I were you, I'd stay out of my way."

Not all educators will be as happy to be in education as you are. And there will be times when you will not see eye to eye, but stay focused on your true mission.

The only way to have peace in the midst of adversity is to silently forgive any trespasses and move on.

When entering a new school, get to know your leadership and operate within those parameters.

"The smile of God is victory."
—John Greenleaf Whittier

Approval Rating

Teresa didn't fully comprehend the scope of her accountability as a beginning teacher. Not only did she seek the approval of her principal, but students, parents, the community at large, and the state all had a say in how well she was doing her job—how well she was teaching.

Trying to please everyone became exhausting and frustrating. If she pleased her students, sometimes the principal wasn't happy. If she pleased the parents, sometimes the kids were disappointed.

There were days when it felt like a no-win situation. She soon learned in her attempts to please everyone, that it was not only impossible, it was paralyzing.

You may choose the road of inaction instead of innovation, just to be on the safe side. Inside you will know you could do more or do better, but you let the approval rating from others tie your hands.

Discovering and doing what is best needs to be your quest. After all, what matters most is that you are serving your students' needs.

Never compromise your principles. Stand firm, and truth will be served.

Do your best and take pride in your decisions.

"People need to see how much
agreement is possible between
seemingly intractable opponents."
—Robert Redford

Satisfaction Guaranteed?

Janice sighed heavily as she hung up the phone. Mrs. Baxter, the mother of a student with special needs, wanted a conference—again.

It seemed that she couldn't please this mother. Although their meetings always ended on a positive note, Janice was beginning to wonder what she could do to avoid them altogether.

This year had definitely been one with unusual challenges in Janice's classroom, and to be truthful, Mrs. Baxter usually had valid concerns.

This conference began just as all the rest—Mrs. Baxter restating her son's needs; Janice restating her desire to meet his needs. But this time, Mrs. Baxter had a new question ready. "What level of satisfaction should a parent expect from your class?"

What a loaded question! Janice was speechless. Mrs. Baxter continued, "We both know that 100 percent is not realistic. Nothing and no one is perfect."

Mrs. Baxter went on to explain that after some soul searching she knew that her own unusually high expectations had created some of the frustrations she was feeling over her son's school year.

Mrs. Baxter's humility struck a chord with Janice. She turned the question around. What were her expectations of parents? Were they realistic? Janice knew she had some of her own soul searching to do.

A willingness to put forth the effort to understand each other opened the door for a wonderful relationship between Janice and Mrs. Baxter.

Make understanding your priority before trying to be understood.

"There's few things as uncommon
as common sense."
—Frank McKinney Hubbard

Mother's Advice

by Ailene Doherty

Ailene's mother had a happy outlook on life that glistened in her hazel eyes and shined through her welcoming smile. In her lilting Scotch-Irish accent, she often offered practical advice.

As a new teacher, Ailene was beginning to appreciate this advice more than ever before. One weekend, Ailene told her mother that her principal was punishing the students too severely. After she had expressed in vibrant tones what she would say to that harsh man, her mother gently corrected, "Little said is easily mended, my dear."

The most amusing bit of advice her mother

had given was "Don't make two bites of a cherry." That is, don't make something more difficult than it actually is. Ailene would think of this adage when she caught herself entering one grade at a time into her grade book rather than waiting until she had corrected the whole set; or when she found herself standing at the copy machine for the fourth time in one day rather than planning to make all her copies at once.

Undoubtedly, valuable lessons in life can be learned through the wisdom and experience of others. Treasure the advice of those who are close to you; they could prove to be your most valuable resources.

Allow your opinions to be enriched by the insight of others.

"I cannot give you the formula for success,
but I can give you the formula for failure—
try to please everybody."

—Herbert Bayard Swope

Easy to Please

With only three years left until he retired, Mr. Latham longed for a peaceful, problem-free year. He was in a school he had led for eight years. This was his last stop. He wanted to leave it on a successful note.

Since his elementary school had more than 800 students, the district built a new school to house the ever-increasing South District student population.

This welcome relief turned into a nightmare as angry parents petitioned re-zoning committees. Latham was flooded with special attendance permits daily, but this was just the beginning of his frustrations.

Long awaited construction at his school had finally begun. However, it displaced many classes and lasted much longer than ever projected.

Teachers were frustrated and parents were even more frustrated. The kids seemed fine. The adults were having all the problems.

Long meetings and lengthy correspondence occupied much of his time. His attempts to please the multitudes were met with skepticism and distrust. At the end of the year, Latham knew it hadn't been his best. Mr. Latham began to wonder if this should be his last year. He thought again and decided that next year would be better. He decided to lead the situations instead of letting the situations lead him.

Upon what gauge are you basing your goals and decisions?

Follow your goals, not the path which follows frustration.

"Kindness is a language which the deaf
can hear and the blind can see."
—Mark Twain

Smile!

by Ailene Doherty

She was about twenty years old, discouraged, and lonely. Maybe she had just been turned down at a job interview, or maybe the young man she was in love with had just told her that everything between them was over. Life was not worth living to her.

The newspaper only stated that a young woman jumped off the Brooklyn Bridge. The note in her jacket read, "If anyone smiles at me today, I won't kill myself."

But nobody did.

She jumped into the swirling waters below.

An immediate reaction upon reading this account is to criticize the people who saw her, but ignored her.

Think instead, *How often do I become so engrossed in my students' passing the Regents exam that I forget to smile?*

Remembering what a smile might have done for that young lady on the Brooklyn Bridge makes us as teachers realize something.

Although your smile may not save a life, it could change a teenager's attitude toward life—even if for only one day.

Your smile could be just what your students need today.

"Facts as facts do not always create a spirit
of reality, because reality is a spirit."
—G.K. Chesterton

George Washington

George Washington's formal education began at the age of seven. Seven was the usual age for teaching children to read and write and to handle numbers. Virginia, like most of the colonies, had no public schools. Most children studied at home.

George's education was a practical one. He learned arithmetic to help him keep accounts and geometry to prepare him for surveying.

He liked to read books that would teach him something useful or give him pleasure. However, his formal education stopped in his early teens. Whatever he learned after that, came from worldly experience, conversation, or reading.

George Washington was one of the few presidents whose formal schooling did not go beyond the level of elementary school. But he never stopped learning from life.

Although you may not be in a position to teach only relevant subjects, try to teach what you have in a relative manner. Answer the question, "So what?" before it is asked. Children remember things that are tied to real life.

Give your students lessons that you've related to current issues. These are the lessons they'll remember the rest of their lives.

Instead of teaching for the next millennium, teach for today.

"Everyone who remembers his own educational experience remembers teachers, not methods and techniques. The teacher is the kingpin of the educational experience."

—Sidney Hook

Celebrate!

Helen felt uncomfortable in a restaurant alone. Since her husband's death, she had avoided going out alone. But today was special. It was their anniversary, and she wanted to celebrate it the way they always had. Her silent reminiscing was threatened by an unusually large group of teenagers. They were celebrating something as well, but they were much too loud about it. And since her retirement from teaching, she just didn't have the tolerance for noisiness anymore.

Helen tried to block out their conversations and bursts of laughter, but it was impossible. She hadn't ordered yet, so she decided to just leave. As she reached for her purse, she heard one slice of their conversation that made her sit back down and unassumingly eavesdrop.

"Can you believe it? We made it! Graduated!" one girl, all in black, said.

"I wouldn't have . . . except for Mr. Baldwin," said another. "I'll never forget him."

"What did he do?"

"He didn't give up on me. Even when I wanted him to," she said. "I'll miss him."

Helen Baldwin's eyes brimmed with tears. They were talking about Frank, her Frank! He was their favorite teacher.

"May I join you?" Helen asked the table of celebrators.
"Frank Baldwin was my favorite as well."

Teach today to be the favorite teacher remembered tomorrow.

"Superior teachers make the poor students
good and the good students superior."
—Marva Collins

Let It Shine!

Dan clutched his principal's permission to start a
young writers' club securely in his hand. It was a
new day! Finally a chance to make a difference
outside the traditions of the classroom. Finally a way
into the hearts of more than just his own students.

The first day of club was overwhelming. Sixty
fifth graders showed up and squeezed into Dan's
smaller-than-average classroom. The fifth grade
teachers showed up as well, most out of curiosity,
but some hoping Dan would fail.

"What's Jason doing here?" one teacher
exclaimed in an indignant whisper. "I can't even
get him to write a complete sentence."

"Look who else is here," another pointed out. "Jessica couldn't spell even if her life depended on it."

The gaggle of teachers laughed loudly, interrupting Dan's opening remarks to his students whose eyes were glued on him as if waiting to finally hear a well-kept secret. His gaze in their direction finally caused the group to leave—all but one.

After three weeks of club, students were asked to share from their writing journals something they were particularly proud of. Jason rose to his feet and began to read. After five emotionally charged pages, his teacher, the one who had remained, was in tears. "I never expected . . ." she tried to say.

"I always knew . . ." Dan said, putting an arm around her shoulders.

Give students a measure of grace, and you will see how much you make a difference.

"The man [or woman] who can make
hard things easy is the educator."
—Ralph Waldo Emerson

The Tutor

Angie Becker soothingly stroked her expanding belly as she watched Jonathon struggle through the algebra problem on the board. She had committed to work with him after school each day for this marking period. It seemed like the only way to give him the extra attention and time he needed to bring up his failing grade. Angie's pregnancy may have tired her physically, but she never tired of the satisfaction and utter joy she felt when Jonathon finally grasped a concept.

Teaching one-on-one in a tutorial way brings two people closer together. Angie felt both pride and affection for this student. He had become close to her as well. But one day, five weeks into their time together, Angie doubled over in pain. In what felt like a frenzy of activity, Angie was whisked away from the school in an ambulance. The last thing she saw was Jonathon's concerned face as he stood helplessly at his desk.

Three weeks later, after the end of the marking period and a less than effective substitute, Angie returned to school. She eyed the pile of work to be graded, and her heart fell as she realized it was too late for Jonathon. As she sifted through that pile, she came upon a plain white envelope. Inside was a card, and on it was scribbled in Jonathon's less than perfect handwriting, "I'm sorry you lost your daughter. But please know you did real well with a son. I got a B! Thank you."

Take the time to make someone else's day a little easier.

"Teaching should be such that what is offered is perceived as a valuable gift and not as a hard duty."

—Albert Einstein

Starting School Too Soon

Danice made the decision to go back to teaching when her son began kindergarten. It was the ideal situation. They would be at the same school! That way she could keep an eye on him and see how he adjusted to school those first few weeks. She had held him back a year because he was a summer baby and she didn't feel he was ready. Now, if there were any problems, she'd be right there. It would be just as she'd always dreamed it would be. Picture perfect!

And it was perfect, for a while. Christopher settled into kindergarten more easily than Danice settled into working full-time again. He acted as if he'd always been there; she felt as if she'd never been there! What was wrong with her? Her signed year contract was the only thing that kept her from resigning.

As it turned out, it was Danice who had gone back to school too soon, not her son. Mounting pressures at home and school made this long-awaited experience a dreadful, unfulfilling one. She admitted to her husband that she had made a mistake, and together they planned for her to stay home once again the next year. It would take careful planning because financially it seemed inadvisable.

Now with the knowledge that she could correct her mistake, Danice was free to give herself to her job and her students. Even though she knew she'd leave them at the end of the year, she also knew that while she was there, they deserved her best.

Give your best, even when you feel your worst.

"The greatest sign of success for a teacher
. . . is to be able to say, 'The children
are now working as if I did not exist.'"
—Maria Montessori

Planned Obsolescence

Michele teaches gifted students at an elementary school in New Mexico. She loves teaching, and it shows. Her high energy is due to a desire to witness and possibly be a part of student learning. She has one great concern. Her students' passion to learn extends only to her own time with them. As complimentary as that may seem, Michele wants more for them.

Her goal? To work herself right out of a job! Her dream? That all of her students, and others like them, can have their needs served right in their regular classrooms. She knows that the state's inclusion program could be put into effect at her school and wants her students to be prepared.

Michele has decided to give her students the tools they will need to succeed, no matter what their learning environment may be. After all, it's not about her; it's about them! Their success will be measured by their adaptability and desire to learn even without her. Just as parents measure the success of their lessons by how their children behave when they are not around, teachers must look for those same results. "I'll be happy when they don't need me anymore—when they can take what's thrown at them and run with it!" Is this really possible? Her heart is right, and time will tell.

You have a telltale heart; it lets everyone know by your actions whose needs you put first.

"There is something that is much more
scarce, something rarer than ability.
It is the ability to recognize ability."
—Robert Half

Diamond in the Rough

Susan began straightening the chairs as the last
fifth grader left her Sunday school classroom.
Looking up she saw Mark at her door. Mark was
the youth pastor, and his face spoke of concern.

"How did Josh do today?" Mark inquired.

Susan lit up! "He prayed out loud for me
today," she said. "He didn't have to say anything,
but he chose to take the risk and prayed for me."

"Did he disrupt the class today?" Mark acted as
if he hadn't heard Susan.

"No. No more than anyone else," she said.

"Then he did cause trouble?"

"No! Didn't you hear me? He thought about someone else today besides himself. He prayed for someone."

She continued. "Josh knows more than we give him credit for. He gave answers I didn't expect and insights I hadn't seen. I thanked him privately for his answers. You know he doesn't like attention called to him."

"No, I didn't know that," Mark replied.

"I know him a little better now," Susan said. "It just takes time."

Upon leaving the room, Mark wondered why he hadn't noticed the things that Susan noticed about Josh. Was it really just a matter of taking the time?

Take the time to get to know your students by heart, not by reputation.

"It is a luxury to learn; but the luxury
of learning is not to be compared
with the luxury of teaching."
—Roswell Dwight Hitchcock

No Substitutions, Please!

Esther is a great school secretary. What she
accomplishes in a day rivals any corporate giant.
One task, however, is especially distressing to her.
When her phone rings at 6:00 A.M., even before she
has left for school, she knows it's a teacher calling
in sick. She sighs in disappointment, then answers
the phone as she prays that a suitable substitute
will be available today.

Why is this such a hassle? Esther knows it is
part of her job description. She doesn't dispute its

necessity. She just knows that today will now be messier than usual and will require her patience. The substitute, if she can find one in time (for they are a limited bunch), will arrive just in time to lead in the pledge. He will then scramble for the rest of the day playing catch-up.

More often than not, the day goes poorly for both the students and the stand-in teacher, and Esther will hear about it. She knows teachers are entitled to use their sick days. She also knows that the teacher's presence brings stability and peace. It's one of the only jobs that is so adversely affected by the absence of an employee. No guilt is intended when Esther greets the teacher with relief upon his return. He is, after all, the teacher—and she appreciates his presence.

Stay healthy—not just for yourself. Your absence affects a multitude!

215

"The gift of teaching is a peculiar
talent and implies a need and a
craving in the teacher himself."
—John Jay Chapman

Art or Skill?

Sometimes beginning teachers are made to feel like beginning athletes. They realize quickly that there is much importance placed on the *skill* of teaching. Make eye contact, conduct a beginning and ending review, circulate the classroom, give enough "think time," and most importantly, use specific praise statements! As Sarah looked over her first evaluation, she felt like teaching was more like a carefully practiced skill than an art.

In this age of accountability, even veteran teachers are relying more on the mechanics of teaching than the artful grace of teaching. After all, one mistake and your school's rating may fall. One false move and your reputation may crumble. Sarah was just beginning to understand the rules of the game. She wasn't sure she liked the rules, but she desperately wanted to play the game.

But even an artist must first learn the skills required of him. Michelangelo had to first learn how to mix pigments as an apprentice in Florence. The mastery of skill gives way to the release of captivating art. Sarah would eventually captivate her students. However, during this apprenticeship, her first year, she needed to learn how to mix her pigments skillfully.

Welcome the refining of your skills; they will serve you well in your artful craft of teaching.

"The place you are in needs you today."
—Katharine Logan

You Are Where You Belong

John couldn't wait to tell his wife the news! He finally got the transfer of his dreams. What seemed like a long time coming was finally here. He would become the curriculum specialist at another school. The only down side was he wouldn't be teaching.

But as John bubbled on about how great this new job would be, he was the one who needed the convincing. "I know it's midyear, but you don't walk away from something like this," he explained. "I know I'll miss the kids, but this gives me a chance to affect many more children."

"When do they expect you to start?" his wife asked.

John knew inside that this was the sticky part. "They expect me in two weeks."

"Kids are resilient. They'll adapt. I'm sure whoever takes your place will care for them as you have."

I wonder, thought John.

The next two weeks were a blur. His students needed reassurance, but all he could do was pack boxes, complete overdue paperwork, and coach the new teacher about what to do and how to do it. This was not how he wanted to leave. It was, however, how he left.

Remember, you are where you are for a reason. That reason just happens to be about four feet tall with two incredulous eyes and lots of questions. Don't walk away until you've met those eyes straight on.

Even in the midst of transition, don't forget the ones you are leaving behind.

219

"A dull teacher, with no
enthusiasm in his own subject,
commits the unpardonable sin."
—R. C. Wallace

What's Your Passion?

"Who was your favorite teacher, Diane?" Julie
asked her friend as they watched their children
play together on the beach.

"That's easy. Mr. Danker, my tenth grade
Biology teacher. He was strange, that was for sure.
But I still remember everything we did in his class.
He was also into taxidermy, and above each of our
desks hung some sort of stuffed animal!" Diane
excitedly explained.

"Oh, how gross!" Julie was horrified.

"No, it was cool. Each week we had a test, and it was difficult. But we could improve that grade if we dared. We could gain extra credit if we ate, without gagging, something he brought in—like oysters, squid, or even pig's feet!" Diane was quite animated now.

"I remember that we created a huge animal collage all through the year. You could only put something on it if you could identify it and tell one defining characteristic. At the end of the year, part of our final exam was to find a particular animal on that collage, identify it, and remember that characteristic. You know, I haven't thought about that in years. Why don't our children's teachers teach like that?" Diane's joy ended abruptly.

Are we teaching like that? Can your students see your passion in what you teach?

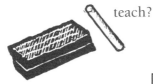

> If you don't have passion, find it! Only then can you light that same flame in your students.

"They know enough who
know how to learn."
—Henry Adams

Vertical Moves

What an incredible semester this had been! Jon had taken two classes at the university toward his degree in Educational Leadership—the principal track. His eyes were now open to realities he never knew existed as a teacher.

He discovered that public education is supposed to be free. Sounds like that is common knowledge, but you wouldn't know it in this climate of the technology race and the desire to provide high interest activities for students. Fundraising had become the unwritten goal of many schools, and Jon's was no exception. He was beginning to wonder about his school's focus.

Were the needs of the children driving their goal, or was it the need of the faculty not to be left behind? They had made up wish lists for parents, solicited from the business community, and started selling advertisements in the school newsletter—all to raise money to get things they believed were necessary to increase student achievement. But were they? Jon wasn't so sure anymore.

Education is costing more and more each year. Unfortunately, student achievement is not increasing at a parallel rate. If money is the answer to student achievement, then what do we say to those in poorer districts—that their children will never be able to succeed? When teachers teach—really teach—students learn. That is the variable most worth investing in.

> Creative teaching doesn't have to cost a fortune. Look for ways to use the resources available to you to enhance your teaching.

"Who dares to teach must
never cease to learn."
—John Cotton Dana

Creature Feature

Carol Dome's classroom was noisy, crowded, and sometimes even smelled! But it wasn't her students' fault—it was the animals. Carol believed that elementary school is a time for exploration and discovery. Creation was up close and personal for her students, and they used any spare moment to observe and comment on their surroundings. The circle of life included them, and Carol's teaching helped connect them all. All except her principal, Mr. Dawsey.

All he saw upon entering her class was chaos. He didn't even know where to begin to conduct her teacher evaluation. He knew the students loved this teacher; he just wasn't convinced much learning was going on. Until one day . . .

The children were unusually reticent and calm when Principal Dawsey entered that day. One of the baby chicks, newly hatched, had died suddenly. Carol Dome was sitting in their midst on the floor, her hands cupped around the now still chick. Each child quietly opened their journals and wrote their reactions to this event. Then one child moved to the bulletin board and adjusted the growth chart of their animal nursery. Finally, another child fetched their book on hatching chicks and read aloud the section about problems during hatching.

Mr. Dawsey saw these children apply a myriad of skills that day, even in the midst of tragedy. Carol Dome's evaluation was a much clearer task to him now. Learning was indeed occurring—even for him.

There is more than one right way to teach.

"I delight in learning so that I can teach."
—Seneca

The Great Adventure

Teachers, on the whole, are an underappreciated lot—until they choose to leave the classroom. Janis left. After sixteen years—ten of which she'd spent at the same school—she left the classroom in favor of a teacher training position.

Reaching as many children as possible, as deeply as possible, was both her professional and her personal goal. Her fulfillment was measured by her success in the classroom. Voted Teacher-of-the-Year two years before, she was at the top of her game. Parents begged for their children to be in her class. Those who weren't were usually desperately disappointed. That disappointment concerned Janis.

She thought there should not be one excellent teacher in a grade—or a school for that matter. There should be many. Janis decided she would encourage all the teachers at her school with newfound strategies and untapped insights she'd learned along the way. Reception of these ideas was usually mixed, but slowly teachers at her school began to look outside of themselves toward new horizons.

Janis, always seeking those new horizons, found a way to legitimately share them with hundreds of teachers in her new position. Appreciation for her talent climaxed on her last day. Amid the students' tears, you could see how deeply she had touched them. She had succeeded!

You may not know your successes or how much you are truly appreciated until you've moved on.

"Those having torches will
pass them on to others."

—Plato

Who Pays Your Dues?

Debbie's new teaching job was in a sixth
grade center in the housing projects of Tampa,
Florida. Not what she had pictured. Not what
she had hoped for. She taught severely learning
disabled students who went home each day to an
empty house, witnessing atrocities she only saw
briefly on the nightly news. How could she
compete with that?

Debbie fully expected to teach well, and she
expected her students to then learn. Her
expectations were both too high and flawed. She
ended up spending most of the year sparring with
them instead—once even physically! All of her

college training did not prepare her for this assignment. Only time and on-the-job experience could have done that.

Many beginning teachers in these situations believe they are just "paying their dues." But their inexperience does not foster student achievement.

When considering a new teaching assignment, it's okay to look for a challenge, but make sure you're not getting yourself in over your head. Remember that it will be your students who pay if you take on a challenge you're not able to rise to.

If you set yourself up for success, you'll also be paving the way for your students to succeed.

"The true aim of everyone who aspires
to be a teacher should be, not to impart
his own opinions, but to kindle minds."
—Frederick William Robertson

Bill Myers - Electrifying

Bill Myers' willingness to learn and be open
to new ideas has made him one of the most
electrifying teachers. As a prolific author and film
director, he is an obvious success. Less obvious,
but seemingly more important to him, is his
success as a teacher. From the Sunday school
classroom to a young writers' conference room, he
imparts knowledge as if he is giving a gift.

Each gift is carefully chosen, attractively
wrapped, and delivered with the anticipated
excitement of the recipient. The gift itself is

priceless advice from an expert craftsman. His generosity generates edge-of-their-seats enthusiasm in his students. Bill, who claims he himself has only about a five-minute attention span, can somehow hold the interest of thirty third- through fifth-graders for hours!

How does he do this? How can *you* do this? By loving what and who you teach so much that your students can't help but be mesmerized by you. Enthusiasm is contagious! And if enthusiasm leads to success, then ask yourself what your students are "catching" from you? If success breeds more success, how are you measuring yours? Bill Myers knows how to light a fire; he just touches his flame to his students' lives.

Is electricity in the air in your classroom? If not, check the power supply first.

231

"The word is half his that speaks,
and half his that hears it."
—Montaigne

Are You Listening?
by Helen Peterson

This was a steady day of testing for Sharon, a special education teacher. Staffings were near, and she needed to finish testing these students. She concentrated on keeping to her schedule in order to finish before the end of the day.

The last student she tested was Sean, a first grader who was struggling to learn.

He began answering the test questions very willingly, but as the session became longer and questions harder, he complained that this was "boring."

Sharon gave him a restroom break hoping that was the problem. But when he came back, he still assured her that this test was "too boring."

Finally, Sharon asked him what he thought the word, *boring,* meant.

"Too hard," he whispered.

Later, as she was writing her anecdotal summary of Sean's testing behavior, she was relieved that she decided to ask him that one question. His report now reflected a more accurate behavior than she had thought initially.

How often do we as teachers assume that we know what children are saying to us without asking the right questions? How often do our students assume they know what we are saying? How often are we both wrong?

In order for you and your students to be communicating with each other, you both need to be on the same page.

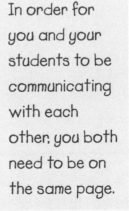

> "Other people can't make you see with their eyes. At best they can only encourage you to use your own."
> —Aldous Leonard Huxley

What You See Is What You Get

As Sarah paces the middle school lunchroom during her lunch duty, she recalls her dad's words. "Make the boss look good," Dad had said. "That's your job." But today Sarah isn't so sure it is that simple. The students are more out of control than usual, and Sarah sees things with her eyes that she wouldn't dare utter with her mouth. Yet she feels her hands are tied. Report trouble or turn her eyes away? After all it's just seventh graders being seventh graders.

It's more than the sliminess she feels under her feet or the elevated volume that's probably a hazard to her hearing. It's the cruelty, the utter disregard for personal space, and the humiliation she witnesses students suffering every day. This is not a safe place to be—not for her or for students.

After lunch Sarah invisibly strolls into the front office. Without even breaking her stride, she picks up an official behavior report form. Back in her classroom she fills in every detail she has witnessed over the past six weeks, then sits back to muster the courage to sign her name to it. It's time to take a stand. She knows it won't make the principal look good, but her conscience is screaming.

Sarah signs and delivers copies to the appropriate mailboxes. What comes next? She doesn't know. But she does know that silence means agreement.

Struggling with an ethical issue? Do the right thing. You're only accountable for your own actions.

"My heart is singing for joy this morning.
A miracle has happened! The light of
understanding has shone upon my little pupil's
mind, and behold, all things are changed."

—Anne Sullivan

The Ah-Ha Effect

Not covered in any college textbook is the
sensation of "Ah-ha!" when a student finally
understands what was once an incomprehensible
concept to him. Judy learned that firsthand when
she tutored a boy diagnosed with a math disability.
It wasn't her student's discovery that changed her,
however; it was her own.

She had learned how to break the learning of a
new concept back down to the concrete level if a
student was having trouble. So when it came to
fractions, a trip to the pizza parlor seemed in order.

Not just because it would be fun, but because Judy herself had always struggled with fractions. Teaching the lesson step-by-step (including consuming the prop) led Judy to an amazing discovery—she finally understood fractions! For the first time in her life, she really understood them! This made teaching them not only easier, but more exciting.

Should it have taken Judy until she was twenty to fully grasp fractions? Unknown. What is known to her now, however, is the power of the Ah-ha effect. She knows that it doesn't really matter how long it takes, as long as it happens. Maybe it will take a different approach. Maybe a student just needs more time. What are you willing to do to ensure your students' success? Your work is not done until you hear, "Oh, I get it!"

Do you know which students "get it" and which don't? You should. Take the time and give more when needed.

"Unless one has taught . . . it is
hard to imagine the extent of the
demands made on a teacher's attention."
—Charles E. Silberman

Homework

"Come to bed," Joe called from the bedroom.
Sally was still at the kitchen table, surrounded by a
mound of papers that held her hostage.

"In a minute," a yawn garbled her answer and
tempted her to bed. "I promised my kids I'd get
these reports back to them by tomorrow."

"Don't you have time to do this at school?" Joe
ignorantly asked.

Sally couldn't believe he could ask this. *How
long have I been teaching? Ten years. Doesn't he know*

by now what this job entails? Obviously not. Just then, a red flier underneath her piled reports caught her attention, "The Great American Teach-In." Suddenly Sally was wide awake with mischievous intent.

"Joe, can you come to my class next week for The Great American Teach-In and tell the kids all about your job?"

Joe agreed. He spent three hours with Sally's sixth graders. Sally enjoyed learning more about Joe's job, and Joe got to experience some of the joys and frustrations of teaching. During lunch he begged off, saying that he'd been called back to work. Sally smiled shyly as she watched her husband pull out of the faculty parking lot.

That night while again amidst her pile, Sally was content, knowing her husband had tasted teaching. She knew he understood now when he said, "I don't know how you do it, because I sure couldn't do that every day!"

Share the wealth! Invite your spouse to school. It will be an education for both of you.

"Educators should be chosen not merely for their special qualifications, but more for their personality and their character, because we teach more by what we are than by what we teach."

—Will Durant

Character Sketch

It was time again for textbook adoption. This year the adoption committee was considering health textbooks. Donna knew that a qualifying indicator for adoption was whether or not character building was included. Donna knew there was trouble when she called the meeting to order and saw the three parents who made up one-third of the adoption committee sitting with their arms folded and lips pressed tight.

"None of these texts represent what I believe my children should think," one mother said.

"I don't see any emphasis on right and wrong. Everything is so wishy washy," said another.

Donna knew she would have to keep her own beliefs to herself, address each concern, and solicit alternative solutions to the problem. Respectfully, she asked each member to write down what character traits they hoped children would learn in school and how that might best be accomplished.

The parents silently but reverently got down to business. Realizing that what they had to say mattered, the parents relaxed, and real work was accomplished. They did not adopt a new health curriculum, but chose instead to integrate timeless truths into every content area. The first line of defense, they agreed, was the teacher. Donna had already modeled that for them.

Character building begins in you, not in a textbook.

"I was still learning when
I taught my last class."
—Claude M. Fuess

Amy Has Left the Building

The day finally arrived. Amy looked around the classroom she used to call her own. Just the box containing the contents of her desk remained. Her last day of teaching—a bittersweet day. Amy soothed her ever growing belly and wondered if this little one would ever understand what she gave up to be with him.

It was as if she were walking through a fog as she locked her room for the last time. Jim, the custodian and one of her best allies, took the box from her and led her down the hallway.

"How about one last turn at hall duty?" he joked.

Amy stood at the entrance of the library and closed her eyes listening for the voices of the sea of sixth graders that filed through that same door each day. But now it was quiet, yet not completely silent. Amy walked through the double doors and into the welcoming arms and voices of her colleagues.

"Congratulations on the beginning of the rest of your life!" The shower surprised her.

At that moment Amy knew that even though she was leaving teaching, teaching would never leave her. Once a teacher always a teacher. Only now she would have the distinct privilege of having a classroom of one.

Even if your days in the classroom are over, your days as a teacher will never end.

"What a teacher thinks she teaches often has little to do with what students learn."
—Susan Ohanian

Just Julie

Julie loved teaching preschool, and the fact that her students were special needs children only made her job more enjoyable. She felt like she was an intimate part of their lives.

Upon meeting parents, she always insisted that they call her by her first name. At only twenty-two, she hated being called Miss Julie—or even worse, Miss Haler. Even her students called her by her first name. She wanted them to think of her as their trusted friend, not just their teacher.

As the year progressed, Julie grew more and more weary of the daily lessons on living. Many of her students were not potty trained, even at four.

But it really wasn't the fact that she had to change diapers that bothered her. It was their unresponsiveness to her attempts to control their outbursts that puzzled Julie and left her exhausted. Sometimes parents volunteered in her class, and on those days the children seemed easier to train.

On one particularly patience-trying day, Julie excused herself to go to her office and regain her composure. What was she doing wrong? Even though she had a parent volunteer, not one student was obeying her. Just as she reentered the classroom, she overheard a parent reprimanding her own daughter, who had been unusually tempestuous that day.

"Alexandra, I expect you to listen to your teacher!" Mom said sternly.

"Why Mom? It's *just* Julie," Alexandra said,

 leaving Julie in shock—yet with her answer.

> Finding it difficult to maintain control? Check to make sure you're still the teacher.

"I am teaching. . . . It's kind of like
having a love affair with a rhinoceros."
—Anne Sexton

Kid in a Candy Store

Linda couldn't wait to show her husband the exhibit hall at the convention. For five years she had attended alone, but this time they could afford to go together. Going into the exhibit hall was Linda's favorite part. She was like a kid in a candy store! Tim spent the whole day trotting after her and holding her various shopping bags.

"You've got to see this!" Linda dragged Tim to the elementary reading booth of a well-known curriculum vendor. "Can you believe it? Finally, a reading program that incorporates writing, but in a way that is relevant and high interest."

Tim just stared at her blankly as if she were speaking another language.

"Isn't this exciting?" Linda could barely contain herself.

Tim snapped out of his confused daze and said, "That's great, Hon. You ready to get something to eat?"

Linda realized, once again, that Tim just didn't get it. Even though she knew that he couldn't possibly understand, she always hoped that maybe this time, he would. She also knew that there was no sense being disappointed about it. What mattered was that she was still excited about teaching. And coming to a convention always reminded her of that all-important fact.

The passion to teach is a unique gift. Even if others don't always understand your enthusiasm, rest assured that they'll be pleased with its results.

"One of the reasons why mature people stop growing and learning, is that they become less and less willing to risk failure."

—John Gardner

Vouchers

by Tony Horning

The teachers at Victory Academy seem to have an enthusiasm and energy about them that visitors almost always notice. There appears to be no difference in this enthusiasm between the new teachers and the veterans, nor does there appear to be any difference in this energy Monday through Friday.

One day Jon Bauer, a visiting consultant, noticed this unique culture and sat with some of the teachers to see if they could help him understand this school-wide phenomenon. The teachers he interviewed on the subject were bursting to tell him all about it!

"It's because of our vouchers," a first grade teacher said.

"Vouchers?" asked the consultant.

"Yes, they're great! You see, our principal gives us a voucher at the start of each school year. The voucher is good for one major mistake per week and unlimited minor mistakes for the entire year. Next year we're creating vouchers for our students, so they can be freed up to try over and over again without fear."

Jon couldn't help but wonder to whom in his life he could offer a voucher. His job was to ensure private schools met accreditation requirements. He wasn't supposed to tolerate mistakes. Yet today he thought maybe instead of a citation, he might write out a voucher instead.

Only when it's okay to fail is it okay to keep on trying.

"If you're too busy to help those
around you succeed, you're too busy."
—Bob Moawad

Too Busy

Elaine's worktable was covered with handouts for tonight's open house. She had some clear goals for both her students and their parents this year. Twenty piles of paper lay on the table waiting for what would bring them all together—the stapler. But where was the stapler?

Students, who just moments earlier were working quietly, slowly began to leave their desks and gather at a far corner of the room. Elaine only noticed in the most academic of ways; for she was totally preoccupied with the task at hand and the elusive location of the stapler. Someone was in need, but Elaine didn't know it.

Finally, Elaine regained her students' attention with a double clap, and all returned to their seats—all but Jason. There he remained curled up on the floor in the corner. As Elaine approached the boy, she noticed his own work lying in a crumbled heap on the floor beside him. Jason held back his tears defiantly as Elaine knelt beside him. "What's wrong?"

It all came tumbling out. "I was trying to put my report in order. I just can't do this right!" Jason surrendered.

"Why didn't you raise your hand?" Elaine asked.

"I did." he said.

It was then that Elaine realized what the more important task was for today—and it wasn't finding the stapler.

The teaching of children should not be sacrificed in favor of paperwork— ever!

"One of the best ways to demonstrate
God's love is to listen to people."
—Bruce Larson

Listen! Do You Want to Know a Secret?

by Tony Horning

James Horner, an elementary principal, has a note pad on his desk. On that pad are the names of different parents, teachers, and staff along with the estimated time he has spent with each one over the course of the past five years. Through these records he has been able to come up with a chart to help him plan his day.

May I see you for just a minute? (Takes about seventeen minutes)

Do you have a moment? (Takes at least twelve minutes)

Got a second? (Takes twenty-one minutes)

May I ask you a quick question? (Takes thirteen minutes)

I NEED to see you right now! (Takes thirty-five minutes—if crying, add another fifteen minutes)

I just stopped in to touch base with you (Takes twenty minutes—if coffee, add another fifteen minutes)

With only so many hours in a school day, James knows how precious each minute can be. Of course Mr. Horner will see everyone who comes by—those who are laughing, those who come in crying, and everyone in between. After all, there is no better way to really share someone's burden or rejoice with them than to be willing to listen with your heart, as well as your ears.

> Listen as though you were going to be tested at the end.

"I have always felt that the true
textbook for the pupil is his teacher."
—Mohandas K. Gandhi

A Lesson in Character

"What beautiful books these are!" Sandy said
after opening the new shipment of character
education books their district had recently ordered.
"Publishers are getting really good at making
textbooks more attractive and user friendly. That's
partially why I liked this series."

"I can't wait to get started," her partner, Janice,
said. "These kids are so rowdy this year. We really
need to teach them about strong character."

Sandy and Janice sorted the books by grade
level and took their own copies to their classroom.
They numbered them and assigned one to each
student. The very next day, they began the first

lesson. They were so excited, they didn't even preview the lesson. They were convinced that this curriculum would make a difference.

The first lesson was on perseverance. However, it took a lot longer to complete than expected. In fact, they were unable to complete their math that day because of it. Frustrated, Sandy skipped to the end of the lesson and gave the students the test. They did poorly. After some discussion, both teachers decided this curriculum was just one more thing they had to fit into their day. "We'll find another way to change their attitudes," Janice conceded.

But they never did.

Want your students to stick to their tasks and finish what they start? Make sure your own perseverance shines through!

"Teachers who set and communicate high expectations to all their students obtain greater academic performance from those students than teachers who set low expectations."

—Research Finding, U.S. Department of Education

Raise the Bar

Chuck taught above average sections of middle school math for fifteen years. He knew what it took for students to be successful in his classroom and was proud of the job he'd done all those years. Then on the last day of school, the secretary asked him to turn in his teacher's manuals because he would be teaching the below average sections this next term.

Chuck laughed aloud as he frantically tried to decide whether or not Mrs. Johnson was joking. Something was terribly wrong. His students had all done quite well. Then why had he been demoted?

Chuck reluctantly handed his manuals to Mrs. Johnson and turned to leave. His principal caught him by the elbow. "Chuck, I'm glad you're up for the challenge. These kids need you. I want only the best for them."

Chuck wasn't sure whether to thank Mr. Cohen or turn in his resignation. Next year would be far from easy. He couldn't depend on his tried and true methods. He'd have to work harder than ever before to reach these kids. And then he realized the source of his resistance and the opportunity this change could give him.

"Thanks for the opportunity, Mr. Cohen. It was time to shake things up a bit. Don't want to get lazy!" Chuck grabbed his new manuals and began to wonder what he could do to create success in his class next year.

When it becomes too easy, it's time to raise the bar. If you're not challenged, you don't learn.

"Woe to him who teaches men
faster than they can learn."
—Will Durant

Follow Those Tracks

Jim Spade watched painfully as one of his students stood facing the blackboard for more than five minutes without even making a scribble on it. Day after day, he wondered what she was even doing in his class. She was obviously not up to Algebra in the eighth grade. Finally, exasperated, Jim said, "Sit down, Miss Downy. Let's give someone else a chance." Jim knew his frustration with this student showed even more than a little. Yet she was in his class, and there was nothing he could do about it. He decided he would not hold up the rest of the class, who clearly belonged there, for this one inept student.

Carolyn Kane read Jim's remarks in the file of this misplaced student. Her heart broke. Where had the mistake been made? She looked at her last year's test scores and found that the student had tested out easily for the advanced math. Yet she was failing Jim's class, and now she was absent at least once a week. It was time for a conference, but not with the parents.

Jim's tightly folded arms told Carolyn all she needed to know. Jim felt no obligation to this student. Her failure was a blemish to him, something better ignored than dealt with. Yet it seemed too late in the year to move the student to the average math class.

Two afternoons a week, Carolyn tutored this student. It was not in her job description. It wasn't her problem. But it was necessary.

Being willing to give a little extra to help meet a student's need is what makes a good teacher great.

"Please remember these two difficult truths of teaching: (1) No matter how much you do, you'll feel it's not enough. (2) Just because you can only do a little is no excuse to do nothing."

—Susan Ohanian

A Test of Fire?

Jane Froman returned to the classroom after a brief, three-year hiatus. She was amazed at how many things had changed in her absence. Upon her return she was handed an oppressive pile of new assessment policies and a schedule for the training that was necessary to make sense of the pile. Jane blinked in disbelief as she realized that school reform had taken them further away from teaching and students further away from real learning.

The new state writing test was a prime example. The state's goal for students on this test, as unrealistic as it was, was tied to their funding. Poor scores equaled a poor school. Jane knew the expectation was that her students needed to score better than the year before. *How?* She wondered, since they were an entirely new set of students?

Her diligence paid off, and Jane's fourth graders did score exceptionally well on the writing test. However, Jane agonized over the myriad of skills she never got around to teaching, since she spent most of her time teaching to the test. Jane wants more for her students. Following her heart will undoubtedly add to her work, but finding that balance is the key to successful teaching.

Teaching to the test should never preclude meeting students' learning needs. Can you do both successfully?

"You take people as far as they will go,
not as far as you would like them to go."
—Jeannette Rankin

The Gardener

Susan learned long ago that not every child will achieve on grade level. Teaching severely learning disabled middle-schoolers gave her a chance to take students far, just not as far as the state was hoping for. By the time students had gotten to her, that fourth grade reading level was probably as high as they were going to go. Instead of looking to see how high they scored on the standardized tests, Susan concentrated on individual skills and learning strategies. She knew they could improve, but she wasn't going to disappoint herself and her students by expecting more than they could give.

"Aren't you being defeatist?" her intern asked.

"Not at all," Susan said. "I've just learned that it doesn't matter how lovingly you plant a seed, nor does it matter how rich the soil is or how well it is watered and fed, some just grow as tall as we imagined they would."

"Doesn't that disappoint you?"

"It used to. But now I've learned to see the beauty of each one, no matter how tall it grows or how glorious it blossoms," Susan said. She knew her intern didn't understand this flowery talk. Those who don't achieve as we hope are not weeds to be plucked out so the garden looks perfect. If you've ever tried to transplant a weed, you know that it doesn't survive. It grows stronger if allowed to stay right where it is.

Set your students up for success by setting realistic expectations for them.

"America's future will be determined
by the home and the school. The
child becomes largely what it is
taught, hence we must watch what
we teach it, how we live before it."
—Jane Addams

Abraham Lincoln

Abe Lincoln got his education "by littles." His formal schooling only amounted to about one year. When he did attend school, it was in the backwoods of Indiana and Kentucky. In a poor school in those woods, no one would notice that his pants were too short, or that he had no shoes. Even though his own father mocked his attempts to get an education, Abe pursued learning regardless of what anyone else thought.

Hard work in rural Indiana in the early 1800's was defined as manual labor, not learning "readin', writin', and cipherin'." Abe was deemed lazy by most in his community. But Abe's stepmother encouraged his learning and made sure he always had a book in his hand. Sometimes it only takes one person to take an interest in a child for him to succeed.

Abraham Lincoln pursued knowledge and truth to the end of becoming President of the United States during our country's most turbulent period. Who would have thought that a gangly boy from the backwoods with almost no formal schooling would become one of our wisest leaders?

Look in your classroom today. You know that boy who comes to school in dirty clothes and is on free lunch? He may have exactly what it takes to make it in this world. You can choose to be his naysayer or his champion.

Some of our students may not look like winners on the outside. So take the time to find out who's on the inside.

"No one should teach who is
not in love with teaching."
—Margaret E. Sangster

Personal Image

This was her first faculty meeting! Amy
scanned the room for a familiar face and found
none. She felt more like it was her first day of
school. Everyone else settled into their seats as if
they owned them. Familiar cliques reunited after a
long, restful summer. "Just think," Amy said to
herself. "We're all here for the same reason. We
have the same mission."

Amy couldn't help but eavesdrop on the
conversations going on in front of and behind
her. She knew everyone must be as excited as she
was to welcome the children—their children.
Amy was wrong.

"Can you believe it?" someone said behind her. "They moved all my stuff just to paint the room! They didn't even have the decency to put it back the way I had left it!"

Then in front of her, "Look at her! She thinks just because she's a dean that she has power over us. It was only a few months ago that she was just a teacher like us."

And then right next to her, "You've got to be kidding! Look at my roster. More than five students in special education. What do they expect me to do? Work miracles?"

Where was the love of teaching? Where was the humility in knowing you would shape young minds? Amy looked in her pocket mirror for the answer. "I hope I never forget why I'm here," she whispered to the image.

When you can't remember why you're where you are, look in the mirror and ask the one who still remembers.

"A child educated only at school
is an uneducated child."
—George Santayana

Whose Side Are You On?

As Karan pens the last page of her book showing parents how to be partners in their child's education, it occurs to her how much times have changed. As a former teacher she understands how important it is for parents to be involved. But she has to smile as she remembers that her own mother never even attended parent/teacher conferences and rarely went to an open house night. All five of her children graduated from high school and college successfully. What has changed?

Karan's passion for education drives her to do whatever it takes to improve the lives of children in and out of her care. She goes above and beyond the call of duty in most cases. That is the message she presents to parents as well. Their influence supercedes her own as a teacher. Their input creates a longer lasting impact.

Maybe times will change again. Maybe someday it will be enough to just drop your child off at school and know that everything will go well. Maybe. But for now, a teacher's job doesn't end when the bell rings. It ends only when those in her charge learn. And at this time, that means forming strong partnerships with parents—being each other's lieutenant! This way you can do battle together!

Not sure where a parent's place is in the education process? Right at your side.

"Nothing fruitful ever comes when plants are forced to flower in the wrong season."
—Bette Bao Lord

Say It Isn't So!

The caller's question made Junetta sigh. So often when she did these radio shows, parents would call in with questions that made her look like a hero. But this question always made Junetta nervous. She knew her answer could make parents angry with her. Yet she couldn't avoid the truth. It would be wrong for her to reinforce wrong thinking.

"My son's teacher wants to hold him back in second grade, but I think she's wrong. How can I convince the principal that the teacher is wrong?"

Junetta chose her words carefully but then said them with confidence. "The truth is that principals discourage teachers from recommending retention.

It doesn't look good on a school's record that they have retentions. But if this principal is standing behind his teacher's decision, I would take heed. She wouldn't made this recommendation unless she was sure."

"But his sister did so well at this school. He can too if we just move forward," the caller sounded desperate.

"I understand your concern, but I am more concerned about your son's future. Just because his sister did well in this school doesn't mean he will. What works with one does not work with another. Instead of forcing him into something before he's ready, why don't you give him the gift of time?" Junetta waited through silence for the caller's reply.

"I never looked at it that way, thank you."

Communicating the truth to someone without alienating them is a difficult job, but the truth will prevail.

"Little seedlings never flourish in the
soil they have been given, be it ever so
excellent, if they are continually pulled
up to see if the roots are grateful yet."

—Bertha Damon

A Matter of Time

The newspaper outlined the governor's
educational reform program all the way down to
what kindergartners should learn by the sixth month
of school! Jean sighed and threw the paper aside.
Some of the proposed changes sounded wonderful,
and the fact that the state actually intended to fund
them was unprecedented. Parents were encouraged,
and the governor was being hailed as a man ahead
of his time. But that was the problem—time.

Three years. The state gave the districts three
years to show leaps of progress. And if they didn't,

they would be shut down! As the elementary supervisor in her district, Jean knew all too well what would follow. She would do everything in her power to initiate the proposed reform. She would in-service her teachers, organize the orders for new materials, and then monitor the students' progress with standardized test scores. After twenty years in this position, she'd gone through these motions at least five times.

Yet things didn't change. In fact they got worse. The students, like young seedlings, may have been nurtured by expert gardeners and grown in the most beautiful garden, but they weren't being fed in the proper doses at the proper times. Most of these new ideas would work, and for some work miracles, yet the state expected results too fast.

> Your methods are like slow-release fertilizers; over time they will produce a bountiful harvest.

273

"It is a mystery why adults expect
perfection from children. Few
grownups can get through a whole
day without making a mistake."
—Marcelene Cox

Who Do You Owe?

Stan was in shock after his annual evaluation.
There were too many check marks in the "Needs
Improvement" column. Since he was on annual
contract, he knew that if things didn't improve, the
school was under no obligation to rehire him. Stan
waited for the principal to remark on his failings.

The principal knew this had been a difficult
year for Stan. The premature death of his wife had
left him both numb and overwhelmed with the
responsibilities of their three children. What Stan
really needed today was support, not ultimatums.

"I know you must feel overwhelmed right now, Stan. I'm personally going to work alongside you to make up your work. In fact, I'll do much of it myself," the principal said.

Stan was so relieved by his principal's kindness. He returned to class with a new lease on life. As his students filed in, he checked the grade book for missing assignments. "Justin!" he shouted across the room. "Looks like you owe me two assignments. I expect them by the end of the day, or I'll drop you one letter grade."

As the student paled and panic swept his face, Stan remembered his own panic about his evaluation and the grace that was extended to him. He called Justin to his desk and said, "On second thought, why don't you come by after your last class and we'll work on those missing assignments together."

In need of grace? Don't forget to extend it to someone else as well.

"School is the marketplace
of possibility, not efficiency."
—Susan Ohanian

Defensive End

Denise couldn't believe she was involved in this kind of conversation once again. *Outsiders have no clue as to why schools make the decisions they make,* she thought. Although even as an insider, Denise didn't know why they made the decisions they made. Regardless, it was time once again to defend the public school system to her friends.

"What I don't understand is why they use a math program that clearly doesn't reach that many children."

"I want to know why there aren't enough textbooks, so my daughter can bring one home to do her homework."

The problem was that Denise had no answers for these questions. She knew that districts made decisions that made no sense to her or to any other teacher. She also knew that she and many others like her had dedicated their lives to public education because they believed they could make a difference in their students' lives.

She answered with confidence, "It's true that there are plenty of problems with the system, but let me tell you why I think the time I give to public education is important." Denise then shared with her friends her passion for teaching and some experiences from her classroom which kept her believing that she was touching lives and that learning was happening, even with the system's imperfections.

The best asset of any school is its dedicated teachers. When people complain to you about what your school doesn't have, gently remind them of what, and who, it does have to offer.

"Light tomorrow with today!"
—Elizabeth Barrett Browning

A Time to Plan

by Helen Peterson

"Congratulations on your retirement," Trevor, a first-year teacher, told Jim. "We are at opposite ends of this career, aren't we?"

"Not entirely. Retirement sneaks up on you very quickly. Have you begun to plan for your retirement yet?"

That question seemed odd to ask such a young teacher. Trevor asked him to elaborate.

"There's so much to consider, it's a shame to wait until the end," Jim began. "First, if you decide to teach in another town or district in state, please consider keeping your retirement plan intact. It's so expensive to buy those years back. And have you considered a savings plan yet?"

"Yes, I started one just this year," Trevor answered proudly.

"Good for you!" Jim told him sincerely. "Another important consideration, then, is this: keep interested in life. Don't let your career engulf all your time. Take time to develop deep relationships and explore hobbies and fitness sports. I read somewhere that you carry into retirement the interests you have nurtured all your life. So you see, you've got to get busy right now. Go for it! By the way, have you signed my book yet, *Oh, the Places You'll Go!*, by Dr. Seuss?"

As Trevor munched on a piece of Jim's retirement cake, he vowed to follow this sage advice.

Remember, it's never too early to prepare to retire.

> Make lesson plans for your students and life plans for yourself.

"If you promise not to believe everything your child says happens at this school, I'll promise not to believe everything he says happens at home."

—Anonymous

He Said, She Said

"My dad says I don't have to listen to you!"

"You can't make me!"

"You want me to do what?"

Day after day, Sandy's ears stung with the words of her seventh graders. She was beginning to wonder what went on in the homes of these students. No wonder kids didn't respect their teachers. It sure sounded as if their parents didn't have any respect for them in the first place. One child in particular, David, shot remarks at Sandy almost daily. A conference was set with his dad for the next day. Sandy cringed at the thought of what she'd hear from this man as well.

A sullen Mr. Rankin slipped quietly into the student desk. Sandy had positioned it so that she could look down at him from her own desk during the conference. Both began the discussion with hesitancy.

"Mr. Rankin, your son is very bright. So much so that it surprises me you've told him he doesn't have to do anything he doesn't want to do," Sandy said.

"That's not how I heard it," Mr. Rankin said. "David says you refuse to help him when he doesn't understand his work."

"Obviously someone is missing from this conference," Sandy laughed.

"I can take care of that," Mr. Rankin said, opening the classroom door.

"Won't you join us, David?"

Make sure all parties are involved in a conference.

"A problem adequately stated is a problem well on its way to being solved."
—R. Buckminster Fuller

Problem Solvers

Nancy's sixth-grade class buzzed with excitement as they worked on their semester project: Find a problem within the school and generate solutions and a plan of action to solve it. Nancy had taken a creative problem-solving class during her master's studies and was anxious to try out the technique with her own students. But the first few days of the process turned into one gripe session after another.

"We don't feel like we belong."

"We don't have a student council."

"The eighth graders pick on us in the halls."

On and on it went, one complaint after another. It was a mess, and Nancy needed to help her students focus on what the real problem was before they could ever consider trying to solve it.

"Let's try to formulate a problem this way: In what way(s) might we _____?" The students then listed all the problems they could think of in this way. After looking at the problems stated on the board, Nancy asked her students if they could think of one problem that narrowed the mess down. They did.

"In what way(s) might we build a sense of community in our school?" Reverent silence followed the realization that they had actually adequately stated the real problem. That was the hard part. Now brainstorming solutions wouldn't be so hard. They were focused and ready for action.

The first step to solving a problem is to be able to state it in a concise way.

"Education is a matter of building bridges."
—Ralph Ellison

There's No Place Like Home

(Written especially for the education
students at Keuka College, New York)

Cassie's decision to teach in her hometown school was an easy one. She knew exactly where she belonged. Yet upon applying, there were no positions available. As a first-year teacher she wanted to be surrounded by family and friends.

Cassie resisted suggestions to apply in the city. But as fall approached and her dreams began to fade, she decided to apply at a few schools in the city.

Within days she had her first interview. She drove the thirty miles into the city and circled the building for fifteen minutes looking for a place to park. The building was old and musty and right in the middle of the wrong part of town. Cassie cringed at the thought of working there.

At the conclusion of her interview, she was offered the position. Exactly what she wanted, in the grade she wanted, but in the wrong place. The principal sensed her hesitation and offered to give her a tour.

"This would be your classroom," the principal said, waving his hand around the brightly lit room. "We're trying to create a friendly environment here. These kids are bussed in away from their neighborhoods and don't feel like they belong. We're trying our best to make them feel at home." At that moment, Cassie realized that she was right where she belonged.

Keep your focus on your students, and you'll never get lost, even if you're far from home.

"There is no influence so powerful
as that of the mother, but next in rank
of efficacy is that of the schoolmaster."

—Sarah Josepha Hale

The Power of Love

Claire walked through the crowded hallway as if in a fog. She was only remotely aware of her son's tiny hand in hers as they approached his kindergarten classroom. The sights, the smells, and the sounds transported Claire back all those years ago to the day her own mother walked her to kindergarten. Where had the years gone? Everyone said that they grow up so fast. And everyone was right. Here was her little man all ready for school. It was a milestone, a day of ceremony and celebration.

Miss Sauri recognized the look on this mother's face even before she was inside the room. This was a face of a good mother, one whose love for her child showed from top to bottom. The trust between mother and son was communicated in a glance. Mom hung up his backpack and then knelt to give him instructions. Her son nodded in complete understanding and then turned to look at Miss Sauri with those same trusting eyes. *Mom has done a good job,* Miss Sauri thought.

Then Claire led her son to his teacher. Taking his hand and placing it in hers, she said, "He's all yours."

"No," Miss Sauri said. "He's yours. He's just on loan to me for now."

> Never under-estimate the power of a mother's love. It's that love that will hopefully be transferred to you.

"Education has for its object the formation of character. This is the aim of both parent and teacher."
—Herbert Spencer

Me? A Teacher?

Chad wondered what his friends would think. He knew that his new job not only would surprise them; it would incite laughter! Chad, a teacher? No way! He never really liked school. He struggled more than some. But after years in a job he didn't train for or like, he knew he needed to change. Becoming a teacher was not his first choice, but it wasn't far-fetched either.

Chad's famed soccer career came to a crashing end when he wrenched his knee. Yet now with surgery, it was stronger than ever. His degree in

science and a love for coaching was all he needed
to convince himself that teaching in a high school
might be a way to satisfy both loves. Midway
through his teacher training, he received a job offer
in a prestigious high school.

"What are your goals for your students?" the
principal asked during his interview.

"I know this will sound idealistic, but I want
them to love science. I want them, for maybe the
first time, to see their connection to this place we
call home. I want them to leave my class intent on
making it a better place to live," Chad paused. "And
I want to be for them what every patient teacher
was for me—hope."

Chad knew it sounded
like a reelection speech, but
he couldn't help it. He meant
every word. For the first
time, he felt he was right
where he belonged.

Those who
can, teach.
Those who
wish they
could only
complain.

"If there is anything that we wish to change
in the child, we should first examine it
and see whether it is not something that
could better be changed in ourselves."
—Carl Jung

On My Honor

Steve cringed when he read the duty roster. In addition to his regular hall duty between classes, he also had to monitor the entire seventh-grade hallway during his free period.

"Just great!" Steve murmured. He knew that most teachers didn't bother to stand outside their doors between classes. He also knew that he was on his own if there was trouble. It would take a fire in the building to get some teachers away from their desks.

Steve watched the corridor for signs of unrest, but only minor infractions cropped up.

"Walk!"

"Get to class!"

"Ladies, this is not a beauty parlor."

Everyday reprimands.

Then suddenly, the hall exploded with voices. Steve made his way quickly toward the far end of the hall. There were eight classrooms in close proximity, but each door was closed to the turmoil in the hallway.

A girl's body was shaking violently on the hard tile floor. Her seizure frightened some and amused others, yet no one moved to help. Steve threw open the nearest door and slammed the call button. A teacher still at her desk looked bewildered. "Student down! Get help now!" Steve barked.

Your sense of duty to your students doesn't end inside the walls of your classroom. Duty is where duty calls.

"Teachers believe they have a gift for giving:
it drives them with the same irrepressible
drive that drives others to create a work
of art or a market or a building."
—A. Bartlett Giamatti

What He Left Behind

Freshman English was a huge class, and seventeen-year-old Jerry Jenkins cringed at the prospect of it. Already he knew that many professors expected students to figure it out for themselves. The fifty-minute classes were drudgery to get through. But Dr. Glenn Arnold was different.

From day one Jerry noticed an enthusiasm and commitment in this professor. The man actually enjoyed what he taught and paid more than just polite tolerance to his students. Dr. Arnold showed personal interest in all of them. He was completely prepared for each class and made what is usually just a requirement the highlight of Jerry's college experience. The class was a living testimony to his commitment. And it was catching!

Years later when Jerry's first book was published, he dedicated it to Dr. Arnold, a teacher whose influence reached into classes Jerry himself taught. He found out all those years later the secret to Dr. Arnold's success.

"My wife prayed for me every moment I taught," Arnold shared.

The circle of commitment was now complete. Mrs. Arnold was committed to her husband. Dr. Arnold was committed to his call. And his student Jerry Jenkins, through his commitment to the truth, was able to give back to his teacher the good things he had reaped as a result of both Dr. and Mrs. Arnold's commitment.

Your commitment does not go unnoticed. It will return to you someday.

"The function of education is to teach one to think intensively and to think critically. Intelligence plus character— that is the goal of true education."
—Martin Luther King Jr.

Why?

"Learn Critical Thinking Skills in 100 Easy Lessons?" Sammie asked. "What kind of book is this?"

"The one from our Critical Thinking Skills workshop, remember?" Judy said with a yawn.

"Even if they are *easy* lessons, I don't have time to teach one hundred of them, do you?" Sammie knew she sounded negative, but she was tired of being told what to teach and how.

"Did anyone think *critically* about including this in our daily lessons?"

"Doubt it," Judy said.

"I have an idea. Let's figure out a way to encourage critical thinking without using this book," Sammie suggested.

"You don't need to tell me," Judy explained. "I've always taught my students to think about why they do what they do, and how to use what they learn in their everyday lives. It's a matter of attitude."

Sammie realized that Judy didn't need this textbook. But at the same time, she knew that she did. "How can I have that attitude?" Sammie questioned.

Judy could see that Sammie was serious now. Concern was written all over her face. "You already do, just by asking the question 'why.' The key is to encourage your students to do the same."

To think critically is not being critical—it's being smart.

"All our children deserve teachers
who believe they can learn and who
will not be satisfied until they do."
—Joe Nathan

Together Forever

Shelly was frantic. Two of her sixth graders
were still failing, even after numerous attempts on
her part to bring them up to speed. Only six weeks
remained until their fate would be determined.

She had tried after-school tutoring, peer tutoring,
and adjusting her teaching methods. These two
students were completely different economically,
ethnically, intellectually, and personally. They only
had one thing in common—their parents' apparent
lack of involvement in their education.

Finally Shelly met with each boy, hoping to gain some insight into his learning styles and motivation.

All Shelly got out of the first student was, "I don't know." Discouraged and still no closer to a solution, she met with the second student.

"Is Jason going to fail? Will he have to go to summer school? If I fail, can we go to the same summer school?" The student flung question after question at Shelly. Then it hit her!

"Michael, are you failing on purpose so you can stay with Jason?"

Michael hesitated but then said, "Someone has to. He's my friend, and now that his dad is out of work, he only feels safe with me."

It explained everything.

"Okay Michael, let's work on this together. How about instead of you both failing together, you succeed together?"

Dig a little deeper and, if you still come up empty, go back and dig deeper still.

"Servant of All is a greater title
than King of Kings."
—F. Crane

VIP

by Tony Horning

They saw him on the school grounds, walking around and looking at the ground as if he'd lost something. Later in the day, they saw him picking up trash around the playground. During recess, they saw him pulling weeds from the flower beds in the front of the school. He was dressed much nicer than a custodian. He wasn't a teacher. Who was this man?

Mrs. Nader's kindergarten class was just beginning to get to know their school, its teachers, and its staff. They'd met Mrs. Ludy, the lunch lady, because she served them every day. They knew Mr.

Foster, the custodian, because he fixed their sink one day. And they knew Miss Dansen, the secretary, because they delivered the attendance to her each day. By the end of the first week, they knew all the important people.

Then on Friday, the man they saw picking up trash and weeding the garden came into their class. He brought their teacher a bouquet of flowers and said, "Kids, you have one of the best teachers in the whole world. I hope you enjoyed your first week of school."

"Who is that man, Mrs. Nader?"

Mrs. Nader chuckled. "That's Mr. Clark, our principal. He cares a lot about our school and wants to keep it looking as nice as possible."

"He sure works hard."

"Yes, he does," she said.

If you think you're a servant, check your reaction the next time you're treated like one.

"There is more treasure in books than in all the pirate's loot on Treasure Island."

—Walt Disney

Never Judge a Book By Its Cover

Joan had gone to great lengths to educate her faculty about the nature and needs of gifted students. Yet every year there was at least one teacher who suffered from elective ignorance. Simply put, the teacher wanted things her way, even at the expense of her students.

Chris was leap years ahead of every other second grader. His parents, after numerous conferences, just told their son to comply even if he already knew the material. But it was hard for him to sit still and quiet all day when he'd already finished his work. After all, he was only eight! He started to get in trouble for being fidgety. He got his name on the board for asking his neighbor a question.

Chris began to bring a book to school to pass the time. His love for science exploded as he read book after book. Unfortunately, even though his time was better spent, his behavior was still in question.

"Did you know that there are 150 different types of jellyfish in the Pacific Ocean alone?" he would excitedly ask his neighbor.

"Shhhhhh!" his teacher said, and on the board his name would go. Chris couldn't win.

Joan listened to this teacher complain about how Chris read in class. She couldn't help but giggle.

"What are you laughing at?" the teacher asked.

"The fact that you have a child who inhales books while most of us struggle with kids who couldn't care less."

Books are never a time waster; they are a time enhancer.

"When you are dealing with a child, keep your wits about you and sit on the floor."
—Austin O'Malley

Floor Show

Pamela disliked what she considered a teacher's uniform. It usually looked like some matronly dress or more often in an elementary setting it was a jumper or denim dress that was decorated with a variety of attention-grabbing paraphernalia. Button covers, I Love Teaching badges, and pins for every holiday and occasion. Pamela wore pants each and every day at her middle school. It was practical and even necessary. It's not that she faulted anyone else for the way they dressed, but a dress would just get in the way.

Sixth graders are a joy to teach. They are still young enough to get excited about learning but old enough to have the skills to produce quality work. Pamela knew it was a challenge to hold their attention at times, but she never ran out of ways to peak their curiosity. This was especially true right before Christmas break when all minds were somewhere else and not on the lesson at hand. Pamela launched one of her most reliable interest-seeking tools.

Amidst the chaos of students settling in after the bell had rung, students stumbled over something on the floor. It was Pamela! She was sitting right in the middle of the room peering into an opaque container, seemingly unaware of their stumblings. Moments later all the students were on the floor beside her quietly waiting for some explanation.

Pamela continued the lesson from the floor for the remainder of the class period. Her students' attention fixed and firm. It's a good thing she wore pants, huh?

Getting down to a student's level sometimes requires you to actually get down on the floor!

"The only reason I always try to meet
and know the parents better is because
it helps me to forgive their children."
—Louis Johannot

TK (Teacher's Kid)

Elizabeth wondered how long she should wait. It
had already been half the school year. She watched as
this fifth grader just barely got by. Being in the gifted
program brought with it certain expectations, and
this student wasn't meeting any of them. Elizabeth
knew that in these cases she was supposed to request
a reevaluation of the student to see if she still
belonged in the program. But Elizabeth was hesitant.
This child's mom was also a teacher of the gifted in
their district and well respected. She knew she'd be
starting a war if she proceeded. Still, she sent the
notice for reevaluation home.

Two days later, Mom, daughter, and the school's assistant principal showed up in her classroom for a meeting. Elizabeth was alone with her conviction. According to the assistant principal and the child's mother, Elizabeth's actions were unwarranted and unprofessional. Although Elizabeth's request for reevaluation was denied, she was glad that she had taken the risk of addressing the situation. Because of the meeting, Elizabeth discovered that the student had some health issues that were contributing to her lackluster performance in the classroom. The student's mom realized during their meeting that she should have shared that necessary piece of information with Elizabeth sooner.

While confronting this parent was anything but easy, Elizabeth felt good knowing that she had opened the lines of communication and would now be able to help this student succeed.

Having trouble with a teacher's kid (TK)? Remember to handle it with grace.

"Happy is the child who has wise parents
and guardians and whose training is
continued when he enters the schoolroom."
—Fanny Jackson Coppin

Perfect Match

Charlie was a teacher's kid now beginning
kindergarten. He was already reading and knew
how to do simple addition. His love for learning
was insatiable and his temperament perfectionistic.
His mother outlined to the principal his specific
academic needs and requested a certain teacher. At
first she was elated to find out that she got who
she requested—until she walked her son to his
class the first day.

The room was crowded and disorganized, even
on the first day of school when teachers try to make

their best impression on parents. Music blared from an unseen cassette player, and those children who had already arrived were either dancing wildly or coloring on the floor. Mom's shock must have been obvious because Mrs. Betts immediately approached her. Charlie, on the other hand, was desperately trying to pull from his mother's frightened grip to go play with the other children.

When he broke free, Mom tried to go after him muttering, "There's been a mistake!" Mrs. Betts led Mom to a table and said, "Your letter helped so much in determining the best placement for Charlie. In no time, you'll see him loosen up and learn to laugh at himself."

And she was right. Mom saw her son blossom socially, yet he retained his love for learning. In fact, it even flourished there. It was a good match after all.

Every one of your students is a mother's child. Keep that utmost in your mind.

"Start a program for gifted children,
and every parent demands
that his child be enrolled."
—Thomas Bailey

Did He Pass?

Rob looked at his list of students to be tested and cringed—twenty-four kids to test in three days! Rob's testing was only the first step in a very long process to be placed in the school's gifted program. Only about 25 percent of those tested would actually qualify for the program. And many of those tested were referred by their own parents. Dealing with the disappointment and sometimes downright indignation of parents was the least favorite part of Rob's job.

Rob could usually tell within the first few minutes of testing whether or not a child would pass his screening test. It was obvious that this second grader wasn't going to make the cut. After testing he met with the parent privately and relayed the results. He could tell from her face. Rob thought to himself, *Another parent who is just convinced that her child is gifted.*

"Please, there must be some mistake," she said.

Rob responded with his all too familiar speech about how this test was not a full IQ test, only a screening instrument and that her son could take it again next year.

"You don't understand," the mom continued. "Mrs. Wickstrom is the best teacher here. She's our last chance to motivate Jon."

It's funny how parents flock to one program or another. It's not because they are elitist or because the program is the popular place to be. It's because a teacher has made it clear to all that kids are important.

> A program is only as successful as its teacher.

"Let early education be a sort of amusement; you will then be better able to discover the child's natural bent."
—Plato

Stand at Attention

When Vanessa enrolled her five-year-old daughter, Kaitlin, in kindergarten she chose a private school. This school had a three-year waiting list, and Vanessa put Kaitlin on it when she was two. She was excited to finally be able to meet the teachers and tour the facility with the eyes of a kindergarten parent.

The rows of desks could not have been more perfectly aligned. Each prospective child's name was displayed on his or her future desk. The bulletin boards were color coordinated with each other, and the discipline plan was in plain sight in the front of the room. Each child had a construction paper bear with his or her name on it. Vanessa read the plan in horror.

Talking out of turn = take bear away

Moving out of seat = take bear away

Dropping pencil = take bear away

No homework = take bear away

Tardiness = take bear away

On and on it went. Vanessa's blood drained from her face as she asked, "But how do they get their bear back?"

The teacher looked at her in disgust. "Not until the next day when it starts all over again." This is the teacher Kaitlin would have in kindergarten? Vanessa politely thanked the teacher for her time and sprinted to the office to take Kaitlin off this hit list!

In discipline, break the will but preserve the spirit of a child.

"The reward of a thing well
done is to have done it."
—Ralph Waldo Emerson

What Do You Deserve?

The disgruntled group of teachers left the retirement meeting disillusioned and disgusted.

"How can they do this to us? After thirty years of faithful service, I want what is coming to me." Cal Walsh had calculated his retirement benefits to the penny. He knew what he had coming to him, and now the district was telling him that there was no money! "I deserve that sick pay!" he ranted to no one in particular as he walked to his car.

The newspaper chronicled the grievances of both sides. Retiring teachers complained that they had been shafted. Administrators cited their contracts and reminded teachers that sick pay was a perk and not a right. It didn't change anything. There was no money. The bond issue had been rejected. Both sides were hurting. Both sides had forgotten why they were doing what they did.

Cal knew that money was not the reason he went into teaching in the first place. He remembered that, to him, it was his calling. Over time though, that calling had become a distant voice, barely audible.

Yes, the monetary rewards of teaching are few and far between. Will you finish well despite the lacking pay? Can you look back on your career year by year and know you gave your best? Can you recall the names and faces of those whose lives are changed because you were their teacher? Even if you can't, rest assured that they remember you.

Your value is measured by your legacy, not your salary.

"Good discipline is a series of little victories
in which a teacher, through small
decencies, reaches a child's heart."
—Haim Ginott

The Play's the Thing

Serena's attempt to fill in for the drama club leader
was falling apart. She'd had no previous drama
training, and even though she'd agreed to do this
out of loyalty to her friend, she was regretting her
decision. The students were unruly at best. They
came to club unprepared, not knowing their lines.
Serena knew her authority was being challenged
and she needed to do something about it fast.

Two of the students who held the lead roles in
the play were especially rude. In fact, they constantly
harassed one student and brought her to tears on

more than one occasion. Serena had warned them that if their behavior continued, she would pull them out of the play. She hoped her threat would never have to be carried out because opening night was in two weeks!

Again they showed up unprepared, and a tearful understudy fled the auditorium before rehearsal even began.

"You made the wrong choice," Serena scolded, and out they went.

Her drama coach friend called her that night furious that her best actors had been thrown out of the play. But Serena's decision stood, and she knew on opening night that it was the right one. The cast gave her a dozen roses presented by the formerly tearful understudy, who that night had the lead.

Make sure double standards never exist in your classroom. Wrong is wrong, no matter who commits it.

"Calming down a noisy, rebellious group of adolescents is a lot like defusing a bomb. Careful, premeditated, calm responses are crucial to success."

—James Nehring

Assignment Alma Mater

Eileen lingered at the locker, letting her fingers brush over the well-worn metallic numbers. Idly, she turned the combination lock and almost expected it to open. Of course it didn't—it hadn't been her locker in more than ten years! Looking down the all too familiar hallway, Eileen Dansk wondered if teaching at her old high school was such a good idea after all.

The first week of school brought with it even more nostalgic memories. Her homeroom buzzed about her presence and the fact that she still looked young enough to be in high school. It was then that she realized this wasn't a dream, but a reality that could easily overcome her. None of her students were in their seats, nor did it look as if they intended to sit down. Eileen stared at the pile of papers she was supposed to get these students to fill out. Her own experience in high school had not been all that pleasant. She'd never felt like she really belonged.

Her ninth graders didn't know that though, and Eileen capitalized on their ignorance. "I have thirty minutes to get you to fill out these forms. If you can do it in fifteen, then maybe I'll have time to tell you what it's going to take for you to really fit in at this school."

It's interesting how the promise of social acceptance motivates kids to pay attention.

> Your own experiences in school can be used to improve those of your students.

"To learn to give up his own will to that of his parents or teacher, as we must to the Great Teacher of all, will surely make us happy in this life and in the life to come."

—Fanny Jackson Coppin

Are You Willing?

"I don't have to listen to you!"

"What will you give me if I do this?"

Karen's head was swimming with the voices of her indignant students. It was the first week of school, and she had already lost her grip on her eighth graders. But then she wondered if she ever had a hold of them in the first place.

Assignments had become bargaining sessions. If you do this, I'll do that. Finish this first, and then we'll do this. On and on it went, day after day. She wasn't teaching; she was begging! Karen remembered that when she was in school, she'd never dare argue with her teacher about the assignment. The teacher had the last word. But not anymore.

Yet she noticed that these same students never seemed happy or content. There was no joy in learning. There was negotiation in its place. Karen had played this game before and lost. It was time for a different strategy.

"I've got a deal for you," she began. "You work, and you'll pass. You don't work, and you'll fail."

Simple yet satisfying.

Break the will without crushing the spirit— that's great teaching.

319

"A problem is a chance for
you to do your best."
—Duke Ellington

Guess Who's
Coming to Dinner?

Brenda watched the documentary about Japan with increasing interest as the reporters attempted to explain why Japanese students scored so much higher than American students on standardized tests. Three things jumped out at Brenda as being possible explanations. They had a longer school day and year. Teachers were highly paid and respected. Parents took major responsibility for their children's education and were very involved. Unfortunately, all these things were rarely found in the United States, if at all. "We are doomed!" Brenda said aloud.

One side note to the documentary captured Brenda's attention. It seems that teachers in Japan are required to visit the home of each of their students at least twice a month. Parents know that the teachers are there to check up on both the children and their parents. Brenda realized that this was one idea she could incorporate. *Parents and teachers always seem to meet on school turf,* she thought. *Why not meet on the family's turf?*

After calculating it out, Brenda figured she could visit three students per week. Her principal was impressed with her plan. It was the parents she needed to convince. After all, they were not used to a teacher making a social call. But how else could she really build a partnership with parents? The challenge was worth pursuing.

> Work side by side with parents. Do whatever it takes to build that bridge.

"There is no shame in asking for help."
—William Glasser, M.D.

Prepare Ye

"How do you really prepare for your first teaching job?" Kal wondered aloud. He finally landed his first job with no time to spare. There were only two more days until pre-service. This was not how he had imagined it to be. He thought he'd be able to spend all summer gathering resources, working through the textbook, and lining up field trips and experts to visit his class. Instead, he barely had time to set up his grade book and number those textbooks.

Kal had the sinking feeling he would spend all year playing catch-up. And that's exactly what happened. He stayed barely one chapter ahead of his students. There was no time for him to plan field trips or devise any high interest activities. So he fell into assigning the chapters, collecting homework, and giving tests. This was not the kind of teacher Kal wanted to be.

For weeks he skipped lunch to stay ahead of the paper pile. One afternoon a colleague stopped by to ask if his class would be interested to join his on a field trip.

"It's last minute, I know. But Mr. Angler's class had to cancel and I need to fill the bus. It would really help me out if you'd come."

Kal's despair turned to relief as he realized the gift this teacher was offering him—a chance to break out of the box he had backed into.

Share your creativity and resources with others. You may be their answer to prayer.

"I had rather excel in knowledge
of what is good than in the extent
of my power and dominion."
—Alexander the Great

Boundary Breaker

by Tony Horning

When Dan Peters became a principal, he eagerly anticipated breaking down the traditional wall between the administration and faculty. After many years in the classroom, he knew firsthand the frustrations and hesitations of teachers. Dan's goal was to create a nonthreatening, safe environment—one that promoted community and produced change. As he entered his office, he determined to maintain an open door policy and build meaningful relationships with his teachers.

Faculty meetings were his first opportunity to build those bridges. He brought new life to those meetings by encouraging participation. But he knew it would take time for his teachers to feel safe enough to take the risk and open their mouths. He also introduced a new process. Once a month, the teachers would meet as a group without him present. Once the meeting concluded, a representative would pass on anything requiring administrative input or action. This gave the teachers the chance to share concerns openly without fear that their supervisor would make a detrimental note about them.

Even though he had every right to be present, Dan chose to create a forum for teachers, new and veteran. He wanted his staff to know that he was more concerned with improving the school than with flexing his administrative muscles.

Have you thanked your principal lately, for the things he or she does to help make your job easier and more fulfilling? If not, make it your priority today.

"An error means a child needs
help, not a reprimand or ridicule
for doing something wrong."
—Marva Collins

Margin of Error

Group projects were always tiresome to
orchestrate, let alone grade. Someone always ended
up doing most of the work. Someone always
became disgruntled. And someone always slid by
doing nothing. Tensions rose and patience wore
thin as students tried desperately to work together,
something to which they were unaccustomed.

Barb had formed the groups herself this time.
They were quite diverse groups, each member with a
unique talent or strength. Each group had their own
topic to study and present to the class. Today was

presentation day. Barb had worked hard to comprise the groups to promote efficiency and quality. It was her decision that was also on the line today.

The first person in the group was designated as the speaker, the person who would present an overview of the project. Group One's speaker rattled off a five-minute overview of their project. When he was done, his group was speechless. The speaker had introduced the wrong topic. He was humiliated, and Barb was furious. How could he have made such a mistake? Barb had made sure each student knew his particular job in the group. They had worked for weeks on their parts.

Upon investigation, Barb realized that the mistake had been her own. She had taught them well how to do their parts. But she neglected to show them how those parts work together.

The next time a student makes a mistake, make sure that it's not your mistake you're seeing reflected instead.

"Why, then the world's mine oyster
Which I with sword will open."
—Shakespeare, *The Merry Wives of Windsor*

Freedom to Choose to Retire

by Helen Peterson

Anna qualified to retire with a good benefit package. However, she really didn't feel ready yet. When she asked herself what she'd rather be doing, the answer was always, "Nothing else." She felt much pleasure in teaching these young, eager students. Her principal and other teachers were her friends. Her life revolved around teaching.

Anna's dedication to her students continued, but new district and state testing made her question whether she was still teaching the way she wanted.

Finally, one fall, whenever Anna asked herself what else she'd rather be doing, she'd smiled and answered herself, "Join a writers' group, read, travel, work part-time in a bookstore, hike, bike, teach adults to read, volunteer in the soup kitchen, go for coffee with my husband, and maybe substitute every once in a while." The list kept growing.

She decided this was the year. She was young enough to enjoy so much more that life has to offer. But she decided to give herself a lifeline, that of renewing her teaching license one more time.

Don't be afraid to move on to another lifestyle when you feel the time is right. Don't feel guilty when you retire. Listen to that different drummer and bask in the freedom retirement gives.

> Retire when the timing is right for you. This is a personal decision.

"Stop talking so much. You never see a heavy thinker with his mouth open."

—George Washington Carver

Lend An Ear

Tori couldn't believe it. She felt just as she had in high school. She had been serious about school, but many of the girls around her weren't. All they did was chatter, especially while the teacher was talking. They commented on so-and-so's outfit or hairstyle. They made fun of those who weren't as popular or as pretty. Tori had become annoyed at these girls who got in the way of her actually learning something. And now, during her first faculty meeting she was experiencing the same frustration.

They were sitting right behind her and spoke in just above whispers. Tori strained to block out their voices to hear her principal. But the distraction was too great, and Tori found herself eavesdropping on their conversation. Believe it or not, they were critiquing the attire of each faculty member. Then they giggled at the bow tie the seventh grade science teacher wore. More high school horrors!

When the meeting ended, Tori nonchalantly turned to get a glimpse of the gossipers. They were picture perfect, dressed in the latest styles with perfectly manicured nails and flawless skin. Tori slipped out of the auditorium, praying that she would be unnoticed, and hid in her classroom.

You've got to be kidding! she thought. *No wonder we don't get treated like professionals; we're still in high school!*

Listen to yourself when you talk. You might be surprised at what you hear.

"Teaching, is not just a job. It is
a human service, and it must
be thought of as a mission."
—Dr. Ralph Tyler

Tell Me Why

(Written especially for the education
students at Keuka College, New York)

Amy was anxious to discover the tricks of her trade. What works? What doesn't? Which method, approach, or strategy would help make her first year of teaching successful? Amy knew that when learning something new, she should ask someone experienced. So when a master teacher visited her campus, she did just that.

"Why?" the teacher asked.

"What do you mean 'why'? Please tell me what makes a successful teacher," Amy pressed.

"It's not the *who, what, where,* or even *how* questions that will get you your answer. Start by asking 'why.'

"As children, the question 'why' is most common and natural, yet we squash it. It makes grown-ups uncomfortable. 'Why' makes a person think— sometimes about things they don't want to think about. Yet in order to improve, in order to reach the unreachable, we must begin by asking 'why.'

"Why does Jane learn fast, yet John does not?

"Why isn't this math curriculum working?

"So the most important question isn't *how* I do what I do," the Teacher continued. "But '*why*' I do what I do."

Write it down, mull it over, but face it today and every day.

Each day ask yourself "why," and then you'll find out exactly what you need to do.

"Every job is a self-portrait of the person who does it. Autograph your work with excellence."
—Erik Erikson

50/50

"He's not pulling his weight around here!" Latisha finally complained aloud. She was tired of covering for Jim, tired of filling in the holes he left in their student's learning. This team teaching thing just wasn't working out. Math scores were considerably lower for all their students. Something had to be done, and Latisha was done doing it herself.

Sitting in her principal's office, Latisha listened as Mr. Balton tried to encourage her.

"I've known about Jim's weaknesses for quite some time," he confessed. "That's why I paired the two of you. I thought he'd learn from you since you are such a good teacher."

Latisha didn't know whether to be angry or thankful. He'd known all this time that Jim was weak in math?

"But I was wrong. First, forgive me for expecting you to do my job for me. It's up to me to make sure my teachers are getting the help they need. Second, don't give up on us, we'll work this out together."

"Well, I'm willing to do my part if you're willing to do yours. But what about Jim's part?" Latisha said.

"How about this instead? You give 100 percent and I'll give 100 percent. Part of mine is to mentor Jim. If we both give 100 percent, the students win!" Balton watched Latisha for signs of agreement.

After a long pause, Latisha finally smiled. "Yes, our students deserve all of me, not just part."

It was a good start.

> Teaching is like a marriage. It's 100/100, not 50/50. Give it your all, regardless of what anyone else does.

"If you plan for a decade, plant a tree. If you plan for a century, teach the children."
—Anonymous

Arbor Day

Ms. Samuels' sixth grade earth science classes were involved in an extensive study of how plants affect their environment. An arborist, a horticulturist, and an environmentalist all came to speak to them about how they might have an impact on their local surroundings. Upon inspection of the school grounds, it was discovered that many of the trees were well over one hundred years old. As exciting as that was, it became quickly apparent that most of them were sick.

The dying trees posed several health and safety problems for the school. Huge infestations of insects lived in them; large limbs were threatening to fall;

and root systems were the culprits of uneven sidewalks. Ms. Samuels was proud of their discovery and presented their concerns to the local school board. Unfortunately, the school board didn't see the problem in the same desperate light they did.

I really thought this exercise would teach students how they could make their world a better place, Samuels thought. *All it did was teach them that it wasn't worth trying.*

The next week Ms. Samuels was called into the principal's office. The principal pointed to the morning's newspaper and asked, "Was this your doing?" The article featured ten of her students and their concerns for safety at the school due to the dying trees.

She smiled to herself, realizing that they learned a way to make a difference after all.

A lesson in real-life problem solving carries students into a promising future.

"Your children need your presence
more than your presents."
—Jean Kerr

Teacher Appreciation

The teacher's lounge began to fill with the aroma of various delectables. Sharon Mazer placed the bouquets of fresh flowers at each table. There were crisp, white linens, good china, polished silver, and even crystal goblets at each place setting. Classical music was piped in through the intercom system. Everything was perfect. Even the fluorescent lighting couldn't ruin the mood of this Teacher Appreciation Day.

Sharon and her makeshift crew of parents led the teachers to tables and began to serve them this lovingly prepared brunch. The teachers were overwhelmed by their kindness. Some even cried.

Sharon couldn't wait until the end of the brunch. She had something special planned.

As the brunch wound to a close, Sharon spoke eloquently about how teachers had touched her life as well as the lives of her children. "There is no greater calling," she said at the end. Then as if on cue, her servers approached each table with what seemed to be a bill in their hands. The teachers opened them with hesitance.

Ooh's and Ahh's exploded from the tables. The PTA had given each teacher a gift certificate to their favorite teacher supply store. The teachers were grateful, but Sharon only wished she could give them more. After all, how could she really repay people who had sacrificed so much just to teach.

Even if you've experienced only small doses of appreciation, know that the world couldn't progress the same without you.

"The real menace in dealing with a
five-year-old is that in no time at all you
begin to sound like a five-year-old."
—John Lubbock

Try It, You'll Like It

Sissy Randolph was grateful for a long-term substitute position in her neighborhood elementary school. Although she preferred older students, she looked forward to taking this kindergarten class for three weeks. How bad could it be?

After the fourth day, Sissy was ready to quit. She had no aide, and keeping up with twenty-five five-year-olds was the hardest job she'd ever had. She spent her day blowing noses, bandaging tiny fingers, tying endless pairs of shoes, and cleaning up from art time, snack time, and playtime.

Her only peace came during nap time, which was always too short. By the time she had convinced all of them to lie still and be quiet, there were only ten minutes left of that precious break. Sissy was convinced more than ever that she was not cut out to teach in the primary grades.

Sissy looked around at the room, much in need of a professional cleaning person. She couldn't leave the room this way. She wanted the regular teacher to come back to a clean, well-organized, and happy classroom. Just as Sissy was leaving, the real teacher returned. Amazed at what she saw, she thanked Sissy profusely as it was obvious she had left her class in capable hands.

Sissy couldn't get out of that room fast enough. *I want my mommy!* she thought as she raced out to the parking lot.

Find out which age you enjoy the most, then go and teach there.

"Some people succeed because they are
destined to, but most people succeed
because they are determined to."
—Austin O'Malley

Change of Plans

It's funny how teachers act like students whenever they get the opportunity, Betsy smiled to herself upon entering the year's first faculty meeting. They had a new principal, and it seemed that half the teachers were ready to give her a hard time and the other half were just silently hoping the life they enjoyed would not change. Betsy didn't like change, but maybe a new principal wasn't such a bad thing.

After polite introductions, the principal jumped right into changes to be made. "Some of us in teaching fly by the seat of our pants and hope that we eventually hit our targets and students will learn. But that rarely works, and I invite you to explore an alternative."

Betsy stared at the blank paper for the longest time, trying to figure out how to do such a foreign assignment. List at least three goals, professional, personal, and community-minded. Then make a plan of action to attain all three goals this year.

I've never thought about goals before! Betsy shuddered. *I don't even know how to begin.* And as if her principal read her thoughts she said, "Start by looking at relationships you'd like to improve, here, at home, with your students."

How much effort do you put into your relationship with your principal? Remember that he or she is there to help you and needs your cooperation and support.

After some thought, Betsy decided her first goal would  be to develop a positive relationship with her new principal.

"A professional is someone who can do
his best work when he doesn't feel like it."
—Diane Sawyer

Inclusion

"So what does inclusion include?" Dennis
asked during a recent team meeting. The fifth grade
teachers chose to give inclusion a try, although each
had a different idea of how to go about it.

"My idea is that the special education teacher
would float between our rooms all day as sort of a
troubleshooter," one teacher explained.

"That's a good start," said another. "But it
would be more helpful if I had her input as I plan
lessons each week."

"True," said a third. "But wouldn't it be great if
she could pull small groups to the side during
instruction and make sure they 'get it'?"

The discussion went on like that for another hour, while Dennis just listened. New to this fifth grade team, he didn't want to make any waves. He had no experience in fifth grade. He had no experience with inclusion. And he didn't want to alienate his new team members, but he had a nagging question that he just couldn't shake.

"Excuse me," Dennis began. "These all sound like good ideas, and it is exciting to think of how they could impact our students, but I wonder . . ."

"What do you wonder?" one teacher asked with warning.

Dennis hesitated. "Two things. One, shouldn't we include the special education teacher in these discussions? After all, it's her job we're making decisions about. And two, what's our part here?"

Silence was the answer.

> When talking about inclusion, be sure to include everyone who will be most affected by it.

"When one door of happiness closes,
another opens; but often we look so long
at the closed door that we do not see
the one which has opened for us."
—Alexander Graham Bell

Holiday Ho-Hum

Patricia's head was swimming with all the information she had acquired from both her diversity and sensitivity training. As a beginning teacher she was especially aware of doing a good job and meeting the needs of all her students, no matter how impossible it seemed. Yet all she could think about that day was how she would celebrate the coming holidays in her classroom.

Her own memories of holidays in school were special, and as a first grade teacher she couldn't imagine just ignoring them as her principal suggested. She stared at the blank bulletin board for what seemed like hours, unable to make up her mind. She didn't want to dictate any one holiday to her students.

"Well, I'm going to decorate it with things that make me feel good," she said and began cutting out construction paper decorations.

"What are you making?" an early arrival asked. But before Patricia could answer, the six-year-old began drawing decorations of her own.

Before the bell even rang, she was on the floor with ten children making holiday decorations for their bulletin board—each slightly different, each just as excited to make this bulletin board their bulletin board.

So Patricia didn't have to figure it out after all. The children had ideas of their own!

Involve students in the planning. It's one of the greatest motivators.

"You gain strength, courage, and confidence by every experience in which you really stop to look fear in the face. You must do the thing which you think you cannot do."
—Eleanor Roosevelt

Under Construction

The announcement was met briefly with applause, but only moments later turned into regret and concern. They all knew construction of the addition and remodeling of the existing buildings was well overdue, but the thought of teaching amidst the coming chaos was not inviting. Principal Lanning and his teachers were bracing for a difficult two years.

The cafeteria was the first to be relocated, and students had to eat in their classrooms. The teachers' workroom was next, and the copy machines and supplies were scattered throughout the remaining untouched areas. Tensions rose, parents complained that it was an unsuitable learning environment. Absenteeism on the parts of teachers and students rose.

Lanning, who still had five years left, seriously considered early retirement. But some teachers beat him to it, and those who remained looked to him for encouragement and leadership.

By the end of the first year of construction, parents had picked up the slack, and the morale in the school slowly improved. When the weather was good, they had picnic lunches outside, and Lanning reinstituted recess. And once a month the PTA dipped into their budget and provided a lavish catered lunch for the teachers. By the end of the construction, they were happy to have survived it, but they were also closer because of it.

A positive attitude is sometimes the only choice you have.

"Every great pitcher needs a great catcher."
—Casey Stengel

First Aide

Joan Steffand's new job as teacher's aide would be a welcome change. The school was within walking distance, and she would be working with a teacher that was well-respected. Days after being offered the job, she was in the classroom unpacking supplies from the summer. She had one concern. The last aide in this job had been with this teacher for fifteen years. How could this teacher come to depend on Joan as much as she depended on her last aide? Joan knew nothing of how this job worked.

"Hi. I'm Stacy Welch. And you must be my answer to prayer!" Stacy Welch immediately picked up a pair of scissors and joined Joan to cut out bulletin board decorations.

"Joan Steffand. Happy to be here," Joan eyed Stacy warily. Was she really at ease as she appeared?

Stacy could see that her new aide needed encouragement. "Joan, I'm so grateful you were available. The thought of beginning this school year alone was not a happy one."

"But you've taught this class for fifteen years. You don't really need an aide," Joan said.

"It's not a matter of ability, Joan. It's a matter of preference."

"But I'm only an aide," said Joan.

"This is our room, our students, and our job. Together we can make a difference," Stacy's resolve swept away any apprehension Joan had left.

Including others in your success is a vital part of creating an atmosphere of teamwork and cooperation in your classroom.

"You can work miracles by having faith in others. To get the best out of people, choose to think and believe the best about them."

—Bob Moawad

Fallen Angel

Cindy listened intently, surprised to hear that her friend had left her job as a school social worker to work in a hospital setting. "But Kendra, you seemed so happy at your first school. You told me you loved the people in the community and felt like you were making a real difference in their lives. What went wrong?"

Cindy had been Kendra's closest friend in college, and had shared Kendra's goal of becoming a school social worker. Confiding in her made Kendra feel better about her choice.

"After that school closed," began Kendra, "I had to take a job in a much larger district. I had to divide my time between five schools and wasn't able to form relationships with the students as before. My whole job description changed. It seemed like I was unofficially in charge of doing all the things no one else wanted to do. If a parent wouldn't sign certain placement papers, it was up to me to go confront them. If a student was physically disruptive in class, it was my job to contact the authorities.

"I started losing the love I once felt toward people. I felt myself becoming cynical and distrusting and began to forget why I'd become a social worker in the first place. I miss working with students, but my new job at the hospital is fulfilling, and I'm starting to feel needed and loved again."

Cindy was happy that Kendra had found a place where she could use her talents, but was saddened by the thought that the school system had lost such a caring person who could have been an integral part of helping students get a good education.

> Sometimes it's the unspoken expectations that drive good people away. Give everyone around you the support they desperately need.

"If you want help, help others. If you want trust, trust others. If you want love, give it away. If you want friends, be one. If you want a great team, be a great teammate. That's how it works."

—Dan Zadra

First Impressions

Sharon locked her car and walked slowly from the school's parking lot to the front office. She stopped midway, closed her eyes, breathed in the crisp September morning air, and impressed the memory. Her first day at her first teaching job— Sharon, caught up in the moment, didn't see the curb until it knocked her down, the contents of her new soft-sided leather briefcase spilling onto the pavement. Out of nowhere a hand reached down to her.

"First day?" Mike said helping Sharon to her feet.

"How could you tell?" Sharon joked to hide her embarrassment.

Once in the office, the secretary greeted her with a smile and a pile of supplies. She balanced her pile as she unlocked the door. Turning on the lights and closing the door, she surveyed the room—smaller than expected. She went to deposit her unwieldy pile and found no teacher desk. Now what? She would also need help carrying things in from her car. Eyeing the office call button, she hesitated. *What will they think of me? I need help already.* Before she could contemplate the answer, the intercom buzzed her instead.

"Miss Campbell, may I send a custodian down to help you set up your room?"

Sharon was speechless. She had been so worried about her own first impression. Look how marvelously this school had impressed her.

First impressions mean a lot. What impression have you made on your school today?

"Nothing great was ever
achieved without enthusiasm."
—Ralph Waldo Emerson

The Power of One

Being a mom, Wyn knew that her attitude and emotional state determined what kind of day she'd have with her family. If she was off, they were all off. What a terrible responsibility that is, to be a human barometer. Even with this knowledge, it took Wyn a lot longer to recognize how she affected her students as well.

There were days when, for one reason or another, she just didn't want to be there. There were days that she never stopped complaining. There were days that she couldn't smile, no matter how she tried. And on those days, her students' behavior mirrored her own. She believed their behavior was out of her control.

One day Wyn received notice that she received the grant she had worked all year on. It would supplement her classroom in a variety of ways. But most of all, it was an accomplishment that reenergized her attitude toward teaching.

In the weeks that followed she approached her job with a renewed sense of purpose and joy. Her students seemed to join in on her enthusiasm, and they, too, had a renewed sense of purpose. The funny thing is that Wyn had the power to change her students' behavior all along. The first step was to change her own.

Wondering why your class seems a little ho-hum? Try brightening your outlook, and see if it is reflected in your students.

"The more you love what you are doing,
the more successful it will be for you."
—Jerry Gillies

Homecoming

Christin cried as she walked out of her school for the last time. Yes, she'd miss the kids. Yes, she'd miss her friends. She'd even miss her mailbox! She knew the tears weren't logical, but they fell nevertheless. Her decision to stay home with her own children was applauded by some and criticized by others. And now as she walked to her car, all she could think about was what she was walking away from. Was it the right decision?

As the beginning of the next school year rolled around, Christin felt disconnected and disoriented. She had never not started school in the fall since before she was five. It didn't feel right. She began to daydream about what it would be like if she did go back. This life felt lonely. It was an unhappy first year at home.

Three years later, the beginning of the school year came and went without Christin even realizing it. She was so busy teaching preschoolers in her own home with her children that she didn't miss the school bell. Sitting with five four-year-olds on her living room floor was joyous.

At the end of one day, one of the moms from her little preschool paused at the door. "Christin, without your dedication, I don't think Jason would be ready for kindergarten next year. I just wanted to say thank you."

If home is where your heart is, go there and find out what work there is for you to do.

"Live your life so that your children can tell their children that you not only stood for something wonderful—you acted on it."
—Dan Zadra

Shining Star

Wolfgang Amadeus Mozart was a young musical genius. It was quite evident to his father from the very beginning that his son was uniquely talented. But he hesitated to teach him too early. He didn't want him to become disenchanted with music because he was pushed too soon. Yet when Mozart was four years old, Papa Mozart had no other choice but to teach his son himself. Already a gifted music teacher, Papa Mozart made his living as the court orchestra leader's assistant. He aspired to become the orchestra leader himself—the only job that would adequately support a family. But that was not to be.

Wolfgang's love for music and his desire to learn was insatiable. When most children groaned at the prospect of practicing for even an hour per day, Mozart had to be persuaded to stop practicing for at least some part of the day. By the age of five he was playing for audiences and bringing in much-needed money for his family. His father was compelled to give up his own dream in favor of his son's genius— the sacrifice of a loving father and teacher.

As teachers, we all choose to put our own aspirations aside for the next generation. Just as Leopold Mozart stepped aside so his son could shine, we must do the same.

Any glory a student attains falls naturally back on his teacher.

"Don't care what others think of what
you do; but care very much about
what you think of what you do."
—St. Frances DeSales

Honor Guard

Dan Shea paced up and down the aisles of his tenth grade English class. It was the last day of their standardized testing. Dan was tired, and he could tell his students were as well. One in particular could barely keep his head up. Dan knew that this behavior meant a low score on the test. This was one of his best students. He cringed at the thought of the repercussions of a poor score on this test.

During their break, Dan consulted with his colleague next door. His advice was not what Dan had expected.

"Dan, you know the consequences if students do poorly on this test!"

"I know. I hate to think which class he'll be placed in next year," Dan said.

"No! It's not the kid I'm worried about. It's you!"

"Me?" Dan was confused.

"His failure is a blemish on your record. Do whatever it takes to prevent that, if you know what I mean."

Dan walked back to his room in shock. *Was he suggesting what I think he's suggesting?* Dan sorted the response forms from the test booklets. When he came upon his sleepy student's, he paused. He scribbled a note and attached it to the front of the form. The best he could do was inform the administration that the student was sleepy. Dan realized then that teachers are tempted to cheat for the same reasons students are.

Honor
above all!

"One person can make a difference,
and every person should try."
—John F. Kennedy

A Seat of Honor

Sally Hill loved her job. Admittedly, teaching in a one-room schoolhouse had a myriad of challenges. They still existed in some black communities. It wasn't just the matter of teaching multiple grade levels or the inconveniences of such cramped surroundings that weighed on Sally's mind. It was the frustration of not being able to give her students all they would need to make it in this cruel world. And little Rosa, as smart as she was, lived with ridicule day in and day out.

Sally knew that showing favoritism toward students was not recommended, but if she could shelter and protect Rosa even just for those hours during the school day, she would feel like she accomplished something. One day the other kids teased Rosa mercilessly, and she began to cry. Sally motioned for Rosa to come up to her desk. From then on, she let Rosa sit up front with her whenever she felt sad.

Rosa Parks knew it was special to sit up front. And when she insisted on sitting up front in a bus in Montgomery, Alabama, she knew that it was wrong that somehow she wasn't considered special enough to sit there.

Sometimes special treatment is the kindest act of all.

"We must travel in the
direction of our fear."
—John Berryman

Leap of Faith

by Helen Peterson

Shirley and her husband had made long-range plans. This was the year both had set for Shirley to retire with good benefits.

Teaching had been a wise career choice for her. Shirley had felt fortunate that she liked teaching, even after that many years. She did have to admit, however, that she'd felt more impatient the last couple of years, but not as burned out as some teachers she'd known.

Financially, she knew that she and her husband had it together. She had aspirations and dreams about next year when she retired.

But, still, she was apprehensive about really doing it. What if she missed teaching too much? What if she didn't have enough to do? What if? What if?

Then, she reviewed the feelings she always had when making major decisions and changes in her life through the years, and realized that basically she didn't like thinking about changes. But after they had happened, she had been satisfied with the outcomes.

As Shirley drove to the district office to hand in her resignation, she felt better. She knew that she wanted to make the leap of faith and retire.

Retirement is a major decision. Consider it well, but then trust that you've made the right decision.

Don't be fearful of change. Take that leap of faith.

"Act as if what you do makes
a difference. It does."
—William James

Glittering Image

Donny Osmond, child star and teen heartthrob of the 1970's, thought he'd learned a lot about life as he and his siblings toured the world singing to millions of die-hard fans. After all, he had a tutor to make sure he was on track. He grew up in a large and loving family and was raised by parents he respected for their dedication, faith, and intelligence. He felt on top of the world until he was a grown man with his own family and life came crashing down.

Donny realized, much to his panic, that he knew very little about real life. He found out that even though he grew up in front of the whole world, he didn't know a thing about living in it. And now, as a father himself, he was determined that his own children would get a real education.

In his autobiography, Donny's concern about a quality education is evident. He says, "I wonder how many former child stars would say they got a great education." Donny missed out on all the social interaction of a traditional school experience. Even though he was always surrounded by people, his lessons were limited to how to "function in an adult world." How detrimental that was for Donny would become evident later in his life.

Sometimes we overlook the child when we focus on his talent. All children deserve a quality education, whether or not they are budding actors, singers, or sports stars.

Whether you're the teacher of a favorite or the famous, give them what they need— not your adoration, but a quality education.

"What will a child learn
sooner than a song?"
—Alexander Pope

The Sound of Music

The Sound of Music was Perry's favorite musical from childhood. As a music teacher, he reveled in its simplicity and grace. He loved music and loved children. His career choice was an easy one. But what of those children who had no talent nor the desire to immerse themselves in the magical world of music? The Von Trapp family singers are a legacy to many. But is it because of their devotion to music or their devotion to one another? Perry knew.

Perry made it a point to meet with teachers from every grade level over the summer. What were they learning that he could put to music and therefore make it easier for all of them to learn?

"After all, we all learned our ABC's that way," Perry explained during one such meeting. By the time school started, he had written songs to teach the states and their capitals, the continents and the oceans, the presidents, the prepositions, and even the categories of animals.

The point of his effort was not to produce a concert of his original songs. It was not to attract publicity to his ever vulnerable music program. It wasn't even to entice students to take up a musical instrument. The end result Perry hoped for, and ultimately found, was that there would be joy in the journey—that the music would move the minds and the hearts of his students.

Use your own passion to ignite the passion inside your students.

"We loved the doctrine
for the teacher's sake."
—Daniel Defoe

The Testing

(Dedicated to the students in the education
department at Clearwater Christian College)

The first time is always the hardest. It's always
the most consuming. And it's always the most sweet.
Teaching future teachers was the most rewarding
work Vikki had ever done. It had a definite domino
effect, reaching far into the future. She laughed
aloud as she remembered her own reaction to this
teaching assignment. *Assessment!* How could she
possibly make such a dry topic come alive?

Twenty-five college juniors and seniors in the
education department of a small private college
had gathered with a collective groan. This was a

dreaded class—one avoided until the very end when students had run out of all other options. All they knew was that it was boring but necessary and definitely hard. Vikki remembered when she herself had taken this same class. It was indeed all they feared. But she didn't want to see fear in their faces each week. She wanted to see intrigue and delight.

She brought them out of their comfort zones of reading, listening to lectures, and taking quizzes and expected of them professional standards, insights, and discussion. She modeled for them what she expected, and they rose to the occasion. The workload was heavy; but the support was strong, and victory was won! Students left her class equipped and motivated. Vikki collapsed with sweet exhaustion when the semester was through. Now she watched as each of their lives touched hundreds more.

When you have a chance to teach teachers, give them what you expect them to pass on to their students.

"From the very beginning of his education, the child should experience the joy of discovery."
—Alfred North Whitehead

Dream Weaver

Mr. Crites was skeptical of his newest student, Neil. Although he was new to this high school as well, he questioned the advanced placement of any student. Most of these students were pushed hard by their parents into situations they were just not ready for. Pride in their children's accomplishments drove parents to skip them one and sometimes two grades ahead. And Neil's records indicated this same pattern.

"We moved here especially because of Blume High School's reputation in the sciences. Neil is both talented and driven," Mrs. Armstrong explained during their conference. Mr. Crites wasn't surprised. Most parents said the same thing.

But Neil surpassed everyone's expectations, even Mr. Crites'. In fact, Mr. Crites became caught up in Neil's drive to prepare for the life he dreamed of. They began to spend every afternoon together in the science lab discovering how the world worked.

Neil Armstrong's dream might not have been realized if it were not for teachers who could see how a dream could be turned into reality.

Forgotten how to dream? Start by dreaming the dreams of your students.

"If you can learn from hard knocks,
you can also learn from soft touches."
—Carolyn Kenmore

Power Up

Brad was warned before he took his first teaching job that those who have the real power in a school may not be who one would expect. The principal's secretary, definitely. The head custodian, most often. The cafeteria manager, many times. But Brad wasn't at all prepared for who had the power in his school—not until it was too late.

At first he couldn't figure out why, after following the directions in his orientation packet, his copies had not been run. Again and again he found them off to the side, out of the pile. He also noticed that his name was misspelled on his mailbox. By the end of the second week, he figured that somehow he was missing some important nugget of information. The workroom aide always seemed incredibly busy, and he didn't want to bother her. But he just needed to know why his stuff wasn't getting done.

The conversation lasted only seconds. This aide had a major attitude problem, one that he seemed to somehow aggravate. An hour later he was called into his principal's office, and there sat the workroom aide with a sly smile on her face. Brad was reprimanded for both not following procedure and antagonizing the aide. He was dumbfounded and speechless.

There were rules here. Rules that a person didn't know about until he had broken them. And the workroom aide was the enforcer.

Brad chose to do his own copying for the rest of the year.

Give new teachers the inside scoop, just as you wish someone had for you.

"We shouldn't teach great books,
we should teach a love of reading."
—Burrbus Frederic Skinner

Just Too Much

The training for this new reading program was grueling. Eve hoped it would be worth it. It involved so much more on the teacher's part for both preparation and instruction. It was definitely not the status quo. Yet, at the same time, it was exciting to break out of the mold. It could ignite a love for the classics she has never before witnessed in students or teachers. But she could tell that her colleague, who also took the training, was not as convinced. It was just too much work.

Eve worked hard to secure the funds necessary for this program in her middle school. In order for the program to accomplish its objectives, it had to be used as prescribed in training. After six weeks Eve was exhausted, but her students were on fire for the classics. Their enthusiasm was enough to keep her going. By the end of the year, she was confident that the program would receive rave reviews from parents, students, and administrators, ensuring future funding.

But the surveys came back unexpectedly negative. Eve couldn't believe that half of the students didn't feel the program was any different than anything else. Half—how could that be? During a meeting with her principal, she found out. The students taught by her colleague were the dissatisfied customers. She refused to implement the program as prescribed. "Just too much work," she admitted finally. And so a dream ended.

Are you a dream maker or a dream breaker?

"The world is all gates, all opportunities,
strings of tension waiting to be struck."
—Ralph Waldo Emerson

Judge Not
by Helen Peterson

Beth had just accepted a full-time teaching position at another school in the district, starting the following fall. Since her current assignment was a temporary contract, she was grateful and excited for the chance to have her own class. She was going to miss the friendships of teachers, the principal, students, and parents here at this school, but she was ready to take on the responsibility and commitment to the new school.

Much to her dismay, when she announced her news in the teachers' lounge, some of the veteran teachers were not elated for her. Instead, they recounted the negative experiences they had teaching at that school. They told her she wasn't going to like it there.

Beth listened quietly to their laments, but in her heart she decided she was going to love teaching at that school. She was going to find the teachers and principal interesting and supportive. She was going to appreciate the uniqueness of each student and teach them well. And you know what? She did!

Being happy and content is a state of mind. Look for the positive in every new change. Don't take the negative from others and assume it's all true. Bonding to a new environment is a challenge that needs to be met. Don't let others' opinions spoil it.

Search for the positive experiences in your journey, and you'll find them.

"Those having torches will
pass them on to others."
—Plato

An Olympic Moment

As chairman for the Special Olympics in her
district, Laura Burns did everything she could to
include as many students as possible in the games
each year. The more the competition, the better the
athletes would be who would rise to the top. As a
marathon runner herself, Laura knew the pleasure
and satisfaction attached to competing in a
challenging event. Then an unexpected honor
presented itself to Laura and her district.

With more than a hundred students from her
district competing in Special Olympics, carrying
the torch from one point to another was especially
challenging. How could she include all her

students in this special honor? As a runner, Laura was asked to do the actual running, and her students could watch. But to Laura, that wasn't good enough.

The day came, and everyone squinted as they watched the horizon for the runner who would pass the torch to Laura. "There he is!" someone shouted and a roar of cheers went up from the gathering crowd. Laura was ready for the handoff.

As the runner neared her position, Laura began running along in a line with her one hundred students ahead of her. When the torch was passed successfully, Laura took that split second to sense the warmth of the flame and closed her eyes in thanksgiving. Then she passed the torch on to the student  closest to her, who ran ahead to the next runner.

You've prepared them well. Know when it's time to pass the torch.

> "The art of teaching is the
> art of assisting discovery."
> —Mark Van Doren

With the Greatest of Ease

Fa•cil•i•ta•tor - n. One who makes things easy or less difficult.

Gwen stared at the overhead and wondered, *Am I a facilitator?* The workshop just seemed more of the same until this issue was introduced. And now she was really wondering about herself. She taught advanced classes, and her students always seemed to be struggling. Her intent had never been to make it easy for them—actually just the opposite.

She thought back over her teaching style. Overheads, lecture formats, note taking for students, use of textbooks and other resource materials—all of it was standard issue in teaching. But did it all "make things easy or less difficult" for her students? Gwen doubted it.

For some reason, she couldn't go back to business as usual at school. This workshop had really gotten under her skin. Finally, out of desperation and hoping for some peace of mind, she did what any good teacher would do. She looked it up: *Facilitate*.

She learned that it means to accelerate, advance, enable, promote, and serve and that it doesn't mean to complicate, discourage, hinder, or obstruct.

Gwen's shoulders slumped, and her head fell. She had wanted to challenge her students, but she realized at that moment that she hadn't been giving them the tools they needed to meet the challenge. That was the day Gwen switched sides.

Which side are you on?

"My idea of education is to
unsettle the minds of the young
and inflame their intellects."
—Robert Maynard Hutchins

At the Movies

Syd left the movie theater amazed that again a
film had been made that touched him deeply
because it was about teachers and teaching. It wasn't
the first time. He thought back over all the films he
had seen in recent years that touched on the
resiliency of the human spirit in teachers—how it
somehow defies the odds and inspires students to
great heights. This film, *Mr. Holland's Opus,* was a
little different. Its focus was on the teacher himself
and his struggles with the fact that he was a teacher
at all. In a society that often doesn't value the

importance of teachers, this film sent a reminder that we need not depend on the approval and accolades of others to validate why we do what we do.

Syd had a hard time accepting the fact that he was a teacher himself. After years in a mismatched career, he took a leap of faith and went into teaching. Against his will, he stepped into this brave new world called school. It took taking himself out of his comfort zone to see the possibilities for himself and students. The realization that this life was a gift was hard to explain to anyone else but another teacher. Syd knew the only course of action was to pass on the torch to his students. That way they, too, could receive this gift and inspire others along the way.

It may seem corny to cry at movies about teachers and teaching. But you won't be crying alone in that theater.

> Passing the torch to your students means setting them on fire for life.

"Good teaching is one-fourth
preparation and three-fourths theater."
—Gail Godwin

Sight Unseen

Mandy eyed the room full of fifth graders and
desperately wished she were somewhere else,
anywhere else! Then to add to her apprehension
she caught her reflection in the glass doors and
cringed at her lack of hair, hollow eyes, and less
than rosy complexion. The chemotherapy had
done its job. The cancer was gone, but the calling
card it left was hard to ignore. What would the
children think? All they would do is stare at her.
They'd never hear the story.

The library was abuzz as the students watched
Mandy walk onto their makeshift stage. She settled
into the chair and unpacked her guitar. Mandy was

sure she heard muffled giggles from the back. She knew that it wouldn't be long until she had their attention, but for the wrong reasons.

After ten minutes of musical storytelling and quick changes, Mandy looked just briefly into the eyes of a girl in the first row. Those eyes were laughing. But it wasn't her patchy hair or the dark circles under her eyes that made her smile. It was the escapades of Scooby-Doo that Mandy spun with her guitar. At the day's end, she was surrounded by students and their questions. But they weren't the kinds of questions Mandy expected. "How do you make your guitar sound like a truck?" Relief flooded Mandy as she realized that they had seen her after all—the real Mandy, not the shell.

Good storytelling is a lost art. It distracts the mind from what is seen and draws it into only what can be imagined.

"At every step a child should be allowed to meet the real experiences of life; the thorns should never be plucked from his roses."

—Ellen Kay

To Read or Not to Read

Tamara tossed and turned all night before finally settling with herself that she would indeed present a certain story to her sixth graders that next day. She knew it was risky. She knew someone might complain. But the value of the story overrode her hesitancy. After all, the classics were the classics, whether a character dies in them or not.

The students were mesmerized as Tamara read aloud. She loved reading aloud, and it showed. At the climax of the story, the main character, a kid their age, died. Everything in the story pointed to that probability, but the students were still caught off guard. A class discussion ensued, and Tamara was so pleased to see that they were really thinking the story through. Their conversations continued well after they left class. And that's when the phone started to ring.

"How could you expose my child to death?"

"How could you read a story where a child dies?"

As Tamara sat in her principal's office, she heard her on the phone with a complaining parent. "Ms. Simpson is one of my best. I have no need to censor her."

Did Tamara regret reading that classic to her students? No. Did her principal regret her reading it? No. Did her students regret her reading it? Not at all. And if it started conversations in their homes about what they did in school, it was worth it!

Your decisions may not always be popular. Just make sure your reasons for them can stand alone.

"We teach more by what we
are than by what we teach."
—Will Durant

Smiley

Mr. Cross ran a tight ship. It was obvious he believed fear to be a great motivator. He tolerated no frivolity and no smiling. Not only did he never smile, he discouraged smiling in students as well. Samuel Clemmens just couldn't stand school because of no smiling. Wasn't life supposed to be fun?

The days were long and tedious. Sam just couldn't keep his lessons in his head. While daydreaming one day, he wondered, *Why is Mr. Cross so cross?* A sly smile graced his face for an instant. In his best handwriting, he wrote an appropriate rhyme about Mr. Cross on his slate, which he easily slid to his neighbor. Within minutes, giggles filled the air, and Mr. Cross's happiness antennae went up in a fury. Scanning the classroom for the culprit, he noticed that Sam was the only one looking seriously at his arithmetic. Curious?

Mr. Cross was the topic of Sam's poetry, the beginning of a distinguished writing career. One never knows how the imagination of his students will be triggered.

There's a chance you will become a character in your student's life story. Are you the good guy or the bad guy?

"There is nothing in a caterpillar that
tells you it's going to be a butterfly."
—William H. Danforth

The Daily News

Glen surveyed his senior journalism class. It had been a long and challenging year. So many of these students had been with him since their freshman year. He remembered their first days together as if it were yesterday. They could barely put complete sentences together, let alone independently run the school's newspaper. He thought that by the end of high school, they would be professionals. But for some reason Glen was still waiting—waiting for these seventeen- and eighteen-year-olds to act like professionals.

No one seemed to be able to concentrate on this last issue. Their minds were filled instead with signing their annuals, summer plans, and summer loves. Glen felt like he was putting this issue together by himself. That's not what he had trained them to do. They had everything they needed to make it in the real world—or did they?

Two years later Glen ritualistically flipped through his morning paper. His eyes fell on the editorial page where a new columnist held the prized spot. He squinted his eyes to be sure he was seeing right. There in front of him was the byline of one of his students. The title of his column was, "Those Who Give Us Wings." The carefully crafted story was about an old journalism teacher who had given this author his wings.

Be patient. Even a butterfly can't fly until his wings dry.

"People seldom see the halting and painful steps by which the most insignificant success is achieved."
—Annie Sullivan

Little by Little

Cheri watched closely as the aide fed Michelle. It was always the same—first the positioning of Michelle in the chair and strapping her in, then the bib, then the introduction to the food placed in front of her. Janice, the aide, reminded Michelle at each mealtime what time of day it was, what she was eating, and what she would do with the fork or spoon. It was a painstakingly slow process, yet Janice was always full of encouragement and patience, something Cheri had been lacking lately.

Her intermediate varying exceptionality class may have been small in comparison to a regular fourth grade classroom, but the demands were infinitely greater. Cheri had been teaching it for ten years, and she could feel burnout right around the corner. Many of her colleagues had already left this kind of classroom. They were always amazed to hear that Cheri was still at it. They weren't the only ones who wondered why.

"I see so little progress," she said to her husband. "I think this will be my last year."

Her principal was not happy with Cheri's news that she wanted to transfer. He knew how difficult it was to integrate a new teacher into this kind of situation.

On her last day, Cheri fed Michelle herself. As she lifted the spoon to her lips, she saw it! A smile! "Did you see that?"

"Yes," said Janice. "And it was all for you."

Cheri rescinded her resignation.

Sometimes just the simplest of steps are enough to encourage us to continue.

About the Author

Vicki Caruana is a veteran educator and curriculum designer. She is author of the best-selling books *Apples & Chalkdust* and *Apples & Chalkdust 2,* along with *Success in School.*

Vicki loves to encourage teachers. She is a featured speaker at conferences for educators in public, private, and home school settings. She writes for a wide variety of publications, including *ParentLife, Focus on the Family, Parenting for High Potential,* and *Becoming Family.* Vicki is founder of Teachers In Prayer for Schools (TIPS), which creates resources to help educators bring about effective and lasting school reform through the power of prayer.

Vicki credits her inspiration to her first grade teacher, Mrs. Robinson at Mount Vernon Elementary School, who influenced her decision at age six to become a teacher, and to her family with whom she lives in Colorado Springs, Colorado.

For additional information on seminars, consulting services, to schedule speaking engagements, or to write the author, please address your correspondence to: vcaruana@aol.com or visit her web site at: www.encourageteachers.com.

Additional copies of this book and other titles published by RiverOak Publishing are available from your local bookstore.

Apples and Chalkdust
Apples and Chalkdust #2
Apples and Chalkdust, gift edition

Visit our Web site at:
www.riveroakpublishing.com

RIVER
OAK

PUBLISHING